Mountain
Harmonies

Mountain Harmonies

Walking the Western Wildernesses

Howard L. Smith

University of New Mexico Press
Albuquerque

© 2004 by the University of New Mexico Press
All rights reserved. Published in 2004
Printed in the United States of America
10 09 08 07 06 05 04   1 2 3 4 5 6 7

Library of Congress Cataloging-in-Publication Data

Smith, Howard L.
Mountain harmonies : walking the western wildernesses /
Howard L. Smith.— 1st ed.
   p. cm.
ISBN 0-8263-3144-0 (cloth : alk. paper)
1. Hiking—West (U.S.) 2. Mountains—West (U.S.)
3. West (U.S.)—Description and travel. I. Title.
GV199.42.W39S65 2004
796.52'2'0978—dc22

                            2003026969

Design and composition: Maya Allen-Gallegos
Typeset in Goudy 11/13.5
Display type set in Goudy Family

Contents

Preface

This book is about adventures in nature, primarily in the mountains, and about how wildness touches the very depth of our being. The experiences I relive in this book occurred principally in the mountains of New Mexico and bordering wild areas of Colorado, but also in the Rocky Mountains of Wyoming and Montana, as well as Washington in the Pacific Northwest. Most of the events happened as I was walking, hiking, camping, and backpacking.

A few of these adventures took place deep within wilderness areas. But, for the most part, they unfolded in spots that are not difficult of access. A wonderful aspect about the simple act of leaving your car behind is that you never know what will surface next, or what enjoyment might be waiting around the next bend. Think of these, then, as uncommon adventures in familiar places.

This breaks a longstanding rule that adventure is only possible in exotic locations, involving lengthy and arduous travel to reach primitive sites that are seldom, if ever, frequented by humans. True adventure implies extreme sports and perilous risk of death. Books abound that replay the daring feats of courageous individuals. Unfortunately, the vast majority of people will never have the opportunity or desire to replicate these travels and the potential for unusual circumstances.

Most of the settings within this book are found in national parks and national forests of the American West. You may have visited the sites yourself. Perhaps memories of similar experiences will come flooding back, enabling you to relive an exciting moment, however brief. With luck, you will remember how acutely attuned your senses were. You will remember the chill in the air, the scent of the forest, the brightness of the sun, and the razor edge you walked between calamity and equanimity.

The stories I tell in the following chapters are within the realm of possibility for most people. You do not have to be a young and cutting-edge extremist to drink deeply from the well of life solidly grounded in nature. Sure, it helps to be young, when you have the strength to hike twenty miles instead of ten, the ability to enjoy a zero-degree night instead of feeling very cold. But youth can also be a hindrance, for the young often cannot be bothered to take the time to appreciate, say, the incredible beauty of a single flower. None of the events in this book involved the Eco-Challenge, technical climbing, multi-day expeditions requiring a legion of Sherpas, or travel to exotic countries designated as high risk by our government. If you are able to walk, or move about in a wheelchair, it is likely that you, too, can feast on such experiences.

One of the important insights that I have gained from these experiences is that a loving connection with nature is decidedly possible for most people. You may not have visited the Bosque del Apache in New Mexico, but perhaps you have visited a local game refuge. If you haven't visited Glacier National Park, you can contemplate such a trip this year. If you cannot afford to travel to the Pecos Wilderness or the Grand Tetons, then you can seek outdoors excursions where you live. You may not be prepared to camp overnight deep in the wilderness, but you have been camping at a state park near your home. In many of these experiences, you, too, can recall special, even funny, events that touched you deeply and made you a better person for having been immersed in the outdoors. The challenge is to open yourself to opportunities for communion with nature in mountains, deserts, seashores, prairies, and other venues of the garden we call earth.

Mountain Harmonies

Walking the Western Wildernesses

La Querencia

The shimmering globe slowly peeked its way over the black outline of the Sandia Mountains, and instantaneously I knew deep down that I had found my *querencia,* or home for my soul. Those who live in this part of the Southwest have a difficult time explaining the comforting attraction we feel for the high, sage-covered desert mesas that drop into gracefully carved arroyos filled with chamisa, cottonwoods, and junipers. *Querencia* is a Spanish word that amply defines our love for this land of breathtakingly high mountain peaks with lush green meadows and spruce forests skirted by fragrant hills of piñon and juniper. Gussie Fauntleroy, writing in the September 1997 issue of *New Mexico* magazine, translates it as "homeland, a place in the heart, the place to which one is deeply drawn. . . . It is the soul's comfort, the heart's joy." As that silvery April moon began to dominate the night sky and billions of twinkling stars winked out of sight, I came to understand that the Land of Enchantment would be my querencia.

We were driving very slowly north on Corrales Road toward a venerable old restaurant known as Casa Vieja. My new friends were introducing me to one of the finer eating establishments on the outskirts of Albuquerque. The old Volkswagen microbus swayed gently through the curves as it followed the country road alongside the Rio Grande. Vegetation was just starting to appear after a cold winter in the Valley. Willows, cottonwoods, and elms were greeting the new season with a slow progression of growth. Like a shy fair maid being courted by a handsome lover, the trees and bushes bordering the fields appeared reluctant to proclaim their intentions or show their favors openly.

I gazed out the fog-frosted window of the microbus across the dark fields and bosque flanking the Rio Grande toward what would become the central symbol of my life and of the lives of many Albuquerqueans— the Sandia Mountains. I did not know much about these mountains, only that they loomed large over the city nestled along the gradually flowing Rio Grande at their base. The west face of the Sandias is rugged, with sharp incisions of canyons falling down from the crest. During the day, from the distance of the city, I could see that the recesses and upper portions were forested, but it was difficult to tell exactly how lush the forests were and how much water could be found down in those canyons. Yet the spirit of the Sandias called from on high and gave me peace. This would certainly more than make do as a new home, I thought.

In the years that followed, my premonitions about New Mexico as a source of sustenance continued to hold true, and they flourished and grew. It is this way for many transplanted souls in the Land of Enchantment, who have also been searching for their querencia and found it here. Some find special attraction in the dry, brilliantly sunny climate. Others are drawn to the diverse cultures that have inhabited the region over the millennia. Many find comfort in the big sky and wide-open spaces where the city sits at the very fringe of the frontier. Still others enjoy the casual, friendly atmosphere of people who display little pretense.

There are a million and one reasons why Albuquerque, Santa Fe, and other places in New Mexico act as a magnet for lost souls. For me the attraction was the unique combination of wilderness mountains and canyons, with easy access to the lofty, cold, snowy peaks of Colorado, Wyoming, and Montana; the ability to luxuriate in little-used red and white rock canyons with meandering clear water and dense streamside growth; the convenience of short jaunts to breathtakingly high mountain meadows and thick dark forests; and the discovery of sacred remote sites in the high desert used by ancient people who, scholars observe, had a much different relationship with the land and nature from that most city people have today.

After settling into my new home and attending to all of the essential but ephemeral trappings associated with city life, I began a series of explorations and excursions that dug more deeply into the marrow of this mountainous land. The sum of these ramblings was more than just a walk in the woods or a saunter along a river course, and through them all I could not help but notice a series of recurring themes and thoughts about people, their relationship to the land, and their place in the order of things.

Jack Turner, mountain guide, philosopher, ski bum, and former professor, expresses this noble idea in his book *The Abstract Wild*: "What we need now is a culture that deeply loves the earth." I couldn't agree more, but I believe the thought can be wisely extended: all people vitally need an intimate connection with the natural world. It is still possible to cultivate this even in an urban society such as ours. Despite the ever-intensifying encroachment of humans on wild places, the conquered wilderness still excites and offers glimpses of our all-but-forgotten heritage.

In the course of my rambles I discovered five essential values that are associated with a love for the natural world and consistent with an intimate relationship with the earth:

1. Sacredness of life
2. Pervasiveness of spirituality (every place has a spirit)
3. Sense of community (rather than individualism)
4. Need for balance and harmony with the world
5. Connectedness of life (everything is interrelated)

I believe that through quite ordinary experiences we can build a deep affection for the earth while embracing these values.

The Sacredness of Life

The sacredness of life becomes very evident in any undeveloped area. A close examination shows ants underfoot, birds coursing through the air, crickets in the distance, gophers burrowing through the topsoil, flies buzzing overhead, and other tangible manifestations of a thriving and fecund earth. We share this planet with a fantastic diversity of life, yet we have forgotten that the operative term is "share." Our definition has become "dominating." As a result, we too often miss the fact that the world is brimming with life.

Early one summer morning I went for my daily constitutional on the Embudito Trail above Albuquerque. My heart was buoyant with the prospects of a fine day. The morning was soft and warm. Enough moisture from the preceding night had formed on the bushes to add a distinctive desert aroma from the Apache plume, chamisa, and four-wing saltbush. Rabbits were about, seeking their final meals before retiring for the day, seeking shelter from others who glided the skies during the day. I looked for coyotes but could see no tricksters in the streambed. It would still be an hour before the sun rose, but already the day was quickly warming.

One

Walking up the dry riverbed of decomposed granite and sand, I found the going tough on the unstable surface. This arroyo has witnessed sudden severe flash floods over the years. In the space of twenty or thirty minutes one of these storms can do more environmental damage than all of the walking I have done, or could do, in a lifetime. The riverbed has six-foot shoulders of sloping sand on each side, with weathered, gnarly chamisa as a reminder of devastation that can occur. Not too long ago this riverbed was six feet higher and those chamisa were not there, until a vast flash flood dramatically altered this flood-plain. I detoured around a flowering datura, made famous in the paintings of Georgia O'Keeffe, and sought a path out of the arroyo.

Ten minutes into the walk I was becoming warm with the climb out of the streambed. The old trail, officially abandoned by the Forest Service but still embraced by the regulars who travel these hills, rises steeply around small boulders and up eroded trail tread. It heads for a higher bench to avoid large boulders, a seasonal stream, and the potential danger that the canyon would hold in a sudden downpour. The path continues with a scrambling climb on loose rock. Rising straight up for four hundred feet, the climb is strenuous, but no one is complaining. This is part of the reason that we are here in the first place.

Winding through mountain mahogany, boulders, yucca, grasses, and stunted piñon pine, the trail drops precipitously down into the valley to rejoin the streambed. The melodious cascading trill of a canyon wren dominates this special enclave as it sends out a message about territorial rights. Rufous hummingbirds are caught in battle, flying high to an apex and then dive-bombing each other. Their swirling sounds fill the sunny canyon. The trail loses one hundred feet in descending to the riverbed, and I begin to catch my breath.

I am walking softly, seeking to achieve a bit of grace at the start of a long day. And then I hear it. There is a slight noise down in the canyon about thirty feet below me. Deer? I take several more steps, and out of the dark green willows obscuring the streambed bounds a large black bear. The canyon walls are about twenty-five yards apart. The bear stops on the bank almost directly opposite from me and sits back on its haunches amid granite rocks and low juniper trees.

My heartbeat returns to normal. The bear appears as startled as I am. It sniffs the air and looks directly at me, wondering what's going to happen next. It is a big solid black bear on the order of two hundred pounds, but looking like five hundred pounds after that sudden scramble. Who is going to make a move? The bear sits there looking at me, occasionally averting its gaze. I do exactly the same.

The bear has calmed down now. I sense that it wants to go back to the streambed where it was munching away on greens. I need to finish my exercise. With a soft *"Mitakuye oyasin,"* Lakota for "all my relations," I let the bear know that I am not a threat and go my way up the trail.

It would be very difficult to argue that the bear and I did not communicate in the ten minutes that had elapsed. It clearly understood that I was just passing through and would cause it no harm. I recognized what it wanted to do and that it would cause me no harm. My hike continued, but with a fullness of life, an incredible blossoming of my senses that is only possible after such encounters. How miraculous is this life, and how abundant with animals—yet bears are seldom found on this trail down so low on the mountain. The encounter had a tangible, sacred quality.

As I reached the point where I usually turn around, it dawned on me that I must once again pass through the valley of the shadow of possible bear death. But the fear was gone. We were just two kindred souls, the bear and I, trying to make our passage through life gracefully. I dropped down to the streambed on my way back to the trailhead. The bear knew my ways and me. It was eating peacefully and did not startle at my return. It would have been a good day to die.

Pervasive Spirituality

A deep connection with the earth ultimately confirms a pervasive spirituality. It is impossible to look upon the beauty of this earth and the heavens without acknowledging a higher power, a Creator, the Great Spirit, or God. Mountains possess tremendous spiritual power. Yet each desert, basin, stream, peak, forest, or other natural feature seems to have a unique spirit. The spirituality of place helps to lift our own thinking to a higher level. People are called softly to a spiritual connection with natural areas and nature. Barry Lopez has poignantly captured this notion: "We often address the physical dimensions of landscape, but they are inseparable from the spiritual dimensions of landscape. It is in dismissing the spiritual dimensions that we are able to behave like barbarians."

One

We had camped for two wonderful nights on the Middle Fork of the Gila River just below an old Indian ruin. Here, in late May, the days started out cool, even crisp in some cases, and then gathered heat as the summer approached. With several recent rains, the Gila was running at a moderate pace, even though it had been a lean year for snow on the high peaks. There was an enchanting bend in the river where the silt-laden Gila paused, pooled, and then glided to another bend. The current was swift but not rushed as it rippled over a rocky bed. We had forded the twenty-foot-wide stream several times in reaching our camp, and the slippery riverbed made these crossings a definite challenge.

In the serpentine canyon, we set camp on a large sandbank covered with tall ponderosa pines and a diverse mixture of willow, box elder, and locust. A well-used campsite with convenient logs surrounding the blackened fire pit indicated that many others had passed this way. The old ruin hung thirty feet above the river in an alcove of the cliff. Sitting by the campfire socializing and preparing meals, our eyes were drawn to this visible reminder of the past, when camping out was a daily reality for the ancient ones. With the ruin looming above, we shared a distinct yet unspoken respect around the campfire. The tales told were a little less ribald. Words were spoken in more subdued tones. The younger folk curtailed their shouting and horsing around.

By the late afternoon, shade consumed the campsite, nestled down in the canyon fifty feet below the rim, bringing sweet relief and enjoyable breezes. The same walls ensured that the site would not see sun until late in the morning. It was easy to understand why ancient ones had chosen this particular place, with its water supply, protection from the elements, and numerous escape routes.

On the last day, I awoke in my sleeping bag to a surprisingly cold morning. What happened to summer? It was way too cold to venture out, so I read a book until restlessness overruled my senses. As usual, no one else had bothered to get up yet to start the stove for hot water or the fire for its entrancing and warming blaze. I pulled on my thick down parka and every last piece of clothing before gathering wood for the fire. Stiffly, I searched for wood at the fringe of the well-used site and realized that we should have gone across the stream to bring in more wood before night set. Cold seemed to penetrate to my very core. It did not seem possible for it to be this cold in the Gila Wilderness in late May. Hours later the temperature would be another sixty degrees higher.

Downstream, the soft golden sun was radiating like a mirage off the walls of the canyon. But to reach this treasure would require fording an icy stream, which did not seem a good idea. Just when I thought that I would have to get back into my sleeping bag for warmth, out popped Dick from his tent to light the stove. Within minutes water was boiling, and, fortified by a cup of hot chocolate, I returned to normal.

An hour later it was time to pack out and head for home. Crossing over the frigid Gila several times, I came to an inviting spot in the warming sun above the sand, round river rocks, clumps of grass, and piles of tangled driftwood. The warmth and beauty of this morning suddenly came together in a most magical and spiritual way. The soft calls of birds filtered down from the treetop canopy. An almost imperceptible breeze moved down canyon along the gurgling river. The air temperature was simultaneously warm and yet refreshingly cool, but not cold. The smell of fecund life filled my senses. For that brief moment, the spirit of the Gila was pervasive. I understood why Indians had been drawn to this sacred site hundreds of years before.

Community

The comforting sense of community and value of close relations with others inevitably surface outside in natural areas. In *The Necessity of Empty Spaces*, Paul Gruchow succinctly captures this idea: "When the earth was still largely a wilderness and the rare thing was a place tamed and made safe for human habitation, there was no beauty or joy of this kind in wilderness." Wild lands evoked threats and insecurity. People clustered for safety and took comfort in the presence of others. Tamed wilderness permitted a full fruition of human relations. Paradoxically, as we use wilderness today to flee the press of a massive population, it is in escaping from others that we simultaneously predispose ourselves to greater appreciation of human interaction.

Sharing nature and wildness with other people inevitably leads to deeper friendships and memorable experiences that highlight our walk through life. Who does not remember the happy moments standing around a campfire in communion with others? Tales are told, jokes interjected, remembrances acknowledged, and fond hopes conveyed as we parcel out deeper insights into our beings. It takes a pretty bleak storm, continuous days of rain, or comrades on the edge of exhaustion not to enjoy one another's company around a blazing fire in the course of these musings. And in the end, we have given our love in the name of friendship and felt closer to each other as a small community.

Clio and I led the troops down a side trail toward Indian Creek dropping off the Pacific Crest Trail in the Glacier Peak Wilderness. It had been a good trip thus far, with ten energetic teens along. Many were new to backpacking. One of them had expensive, heavy, and wonderful leather boots that had not been properly worn in. I carried them for her as she limped down the trail behind me. Later that afternoon Clio would start the stove and bring water to a boil so that we could clean out another teen's infected blisters before administering first aid. The two teens' packs had been lightened as we distributed the load among ourselves and shared the burden of their pain.

We quickly adapted to each other's peculiarities. At breakfast each of the young folk cautiously but quickly took a share of the meal before backing well away to the warmth of the fire. Three days earlier Clio had firmly announced that few things bothered him more than people who lingered around the communal pots, making it difficult for others to get their share. He only had to say that once. The teens only needed to be told it once. New to the wilderness, they were as anxious as we were for the comfort of the group.

After several days and nights under Glacier Peak's charm, we headed down Indian Creek to the White River. We lingered along the trail throughout the morning, enjoying great vistas of Glacier Peak and its handsome, rugged features of rock and snow. The day was sunny and warm, with light breezes flowing over the crest. To the west we could see clouds—a typical view in the Cascades. Tonight it would rain, but for this moment we reveled in almost inconceivable beauty.

The Crest Trail had been littered with lovely little tarns that spoke volumes about winter and reality on the Cascade Crest. Wildflowers were beyond abundant—pasque flowers, lupine, marigolds, Indian paintbrush, yarrow. Magenta, soft yellow, and purple-blue flowers greeted us as we wound along the trail. The profusion of colors, buds, petals, and flowers was overwhelming. For much of the year, we contemplate visiting the mountains for just such an explosion. But one must be lucky. A single week earlier or later makes all the difference in the world in the alpine country. Even the teens, normally so absorbed in themselves, were mesmerized by the profusion of color and beauty.

Clio stopped to make certain that all of the party knew to turn left off the trail, but by now we were all acutely sensitive to the pace and presence of our family. Within minutes the group reassembled and was ready to make the final hike to this night's camp. Down into subalpine terrain the trail switchbacked until large forested areas dominated. It was sad to leave the vistas and light of the crest behind, having fought hard for the elevation gain.

Still high on the mountain, but in a copse of fir trees, we found a likely site for our camp. With the large party we needed plenty of space. Clio and I were out ahead of the rest, so we wiggled out of our packs and began to assess this site as our home for the evening. Clio began to meander off to the western fringe of the site, looking intently at the ground. "Hey, Howard. You'll want to take a look at this," he said. I stopped my search for firewood and walked in his direction.

Clio was staring at a scene of great devastation. I wandered over to see what had riveted his attention. There, in an area measuring about twenty feet by twenty feet, was a massive plot of highly disturbed soil. Shallow roots and clods of earth were flung everywhere. Even Clio's rototiller could not have done a better job in turning over the soil. We looked at each other with eyes wide open. Black bears generally do not root up ground like this. We knew that grizzly bear sightings had been confirmed just over the wilderness boundary in North Cascades National Park and on the Canadian border.

Neither Clio nor I slept much that night. We were the elders and responsible for this great group of young people. We didn't say a word about the devastation and its implications. The teens all slept very well that night after a superb meal and lots of fireside banter. They would continue to replay the tales of funny events, sorrows about physical stresses, laughter about quality and adequacy of the meals, and their lessons about sharing in the wilds with others. Clio and I would be forever bonded by that night of sleepless vigil thinking about the safety of our friends, the community that had magically evolved, and the adventure that we had not anticipated.

Harmony and Balance

In Navajo culture, a number of ceremonies exist for protection, thanksgiving, blessing, purification, and so forth. These ceremonies are termed "Ways," as in the Blessing Way or the Enemy Way. The central idea of a Way is to bring a person back into harmony with the natural world. A complex belief system surrounds the notion of harmony or balance, called *họzhọ*. There is enormous rationale for applying the concepts of harmony and balance to contemporary life as a matter of daily celebration. If we are out of harmony with our spirituality, mental and physical being, and environment (especially others around us), then imbalance occurs, and with this imbalance comes stress. The imperative is to gain our *họzhọ* as quickly as possible.

Seldom does a trip to wild country, even an undeveloped lot in the middle of the city, fail to accentuate the importance of regaining harmony with the earth. Wilderness and natural areas inevitably remind us of the natural flow of life and what is important in the greater scheme of things. Not surprisingly, it is the abundance of life and its perfect interplay that inspires a sense of awe and understanding of nature and harmony. So-called civilization with its great comforts and contributions is intoxicating, but it separates people from the natural order and rhythms of this earth. Cut off from wildness, we lose harmony with the earth and degenerate into something not truly alive.

In a long horseback ride across New Mexico that often removed him for days at a time from people and towns, Douglas Preston eventually ran smack into the largest metropolitan area. Recorded in his book Cities of Gold, his words echo a lament for our loss of harmony with the land:

> Never in my life had I been so repelled by the ugliness, the bizarre grotesqueness, of the city. It wasn't Albuquerque itself. Rather it was the shock of arriving so unprepared at the city's stinking underbelly; it was the shock of coming upon three hundred thousand people after having seen not one single human being since leaving Acoma Pueblo; but most of all it was the shock of seeing the city in a completely different context. It was a classic case of jamais vu; here I had spent ten years in Manhattan, but never had I seen so clearly the hideous, repulsive, depraved, malefic character of the city.

Preston makes the significant point that we do not even realize how far out of harmony we are, given the confines of city life.

As the fall season began to take hold with shorter days and plummeting temperatures, the camping days were clearly numbered for the year. One weekend, despite a very pressing agenda of totally meaningless professional assignments that still needed to be completed, we decided to go car camping in the Pecos Wilderness. I could not break free until after noon on Saturday, and I really needed to be home before noon on Sunday as a compromise for the work demands. But a night camping was better than no night camping. To shorten the drive, we selected the Pecos Wilderness.

Having worked hard on various assignments all Saturday morning, I took off for the Pecos Wilderness at 2:00 p.m., looking forward to meeting my friends Bill and Terrye. I sped along the freeway making great time to Glorieta and the turnoff to the town of Pecos. Traffic then slowed to a crawl because of all the families out for a leisurely drive. In retrospect this change was like a salve—it allowed me to detune after barreling up the interstate at seventy-five miles per hour. In the back of my mind I caught a glimpse of a thought about harmony and balance. This feeling only intensified in driving slowly along the Pecos River. I had forgotten how beautiful it could be.

At a bridge crossing the Pecos, I turned west toward the campground. The bridge has lots of character, and its rustic quality serves as a visible reminder and symbol that wilderness is at hand. As it wound through the forest, trees covered the road with their shade and life. I came upon two all-terrain vehicles overloaded with passengers. Following slowly behind until they pulled to the side, I was dismayed by the adult toys. When I reached the campground one-half mile farther along I was mortified.

What should have been an almost empty campground was filled to the brim with trailers, muscle trucks, and all-terrain vehicles. We had hoped to beat rifle-hunting season, but the bow-hunters were out in force. I drove dejectedly up the crowded campground looking for Bill and Terrye's vehicle. There was nary an open site. Then I found their truck and became severely depressed, enough to think about going back home.

Each campsite on either side of us had large families. To the north the family had a huge party tent and many smaller tents. Worse yet, they had a boom box going, and it wasn't playing my song. They would undoubtedly be up all night with revelry. At the site across from us, hunters had set up a practice range for target shooting.

I walked up the road to the trailhead searching for Bill and Terrye. After only half a mile they came gliding down the trail with big smiles on their faces. A walk in the woods had clearly helped to restore their harmony. Terrye was quick to pick up on my displeasure and suggested moving to the walk-in campsites. I had not even noticed them in my huff. Bless the Forest Service! At the upper end of the campground behind two small hills were several walk-in sites, where you had to carry your gear perhaps forty yards to a fire-ring, table, and tent pad.

I could almost feel my relaxation and return to balance with this fringe of the wilderness. What a difference these sites made. It was as if we were in another part of the forest. Only if we looked very carefully could we detect any light or campfire from the urban village below our spot above the two protective hills. Without the intrusion of machines and people, we settled into enjoying the forest and camaraderie around the blazing juniper fire.

We had an absolutely great camp that gave the impression that we were miles into the Pecos Wilderness by ourselves. The fire was toasty and allowed us to converse about things large and small. We fell into the rhythm of the mountains. Stepping away from the fire provided an encompassing view of the stars and reminded us of a grander cosmic order. The next morning we had another fine fire and tasty breakfast before a beautiful walk in the Pecos. But what we took back most from this experience was a return to balance with the land—if only for a moment—that would serve as a reminder of who we fundamentally are and what we truly value.

Connectedness of Life

A final value that surfaces from time spent intimately with nature is the connectedness of life. Everything is interrelated. As our scientific knowledge of nature matured, we developed the concept of ecosystems to capture the fact accurately that mountains, watersheds, rivers, air, forests, and flora and fauna are inexorably tied together. You cannot save a stand of trees without attending to all of the other ingredients that support the stand. John Muir poignantly captured this interconnectedness with his famous quote, from *My First Summer in the Sierra*, that "When we try to pick out anything by itself, we find it hitched to everything else in the universe." What a marvelous thought that moves from the abstract to reality every time you walk along a mountain path.

La Querencia

❋ ❋ ❋

Last summer when visiting the Valley of the Ten Peaks above Banff, Canada, I christened the day by hiking up the trail toward one of the high mountain passes. Beginning at the jade green Moraine Lake, a classic glacial-fed lake, the trail passes several crystal-clear streams as it switchbacks up the tree-covered mountainside. By starting early, I hoped to increase the chance of seeing wildlife, particularly a grizzly bear. As I made my way up to subalpine country, my sense of wildness and solitude heightened. Walking alone through copses of stunted spruce trees where the view of the trail was obscured confirmed the wilderness aspects of the Canadian Rockies and sharpened my senses to a razor's edge.

I never did see the great bear. But I did see the soft morning light upon green avalanche slopes. I saw streams of the purest water flowing from ice melt. I saw low-growing flowers that survived another frigid night. I saw rocky spires swathed in mist and cloud. I saw glaciers laid bare by the summer sun that within weeks would begin the process of regeneration with the fall season. I saw forests whose trees shed needles, bark, and limbs before falling to the floor as supplement to enrich the soil. I saw trees that provided homes for birds and food for bear, elk, and deer. I saw the absence of people and the silence that results. I saw clouds floating across the sky, dancing along like Spanish galleons on the sea. I saw the great mystery that is earth and life that dwells upon it. And I saw how it all comes together in good measure and perfect relation to the separate parts. This was the interconnection of things that we lose sight of in city life, a tapestry of fragile interrelationships.

The
Sacredness
of Life

Spirits in the Sandias

The world is brimming with a fantastic abundance of life, and unless we look a little closer with wonder and awe, we can take it for granted. As children, we are fascinated with the many different types of animals that inhabit the earth. But somewhere along in the transition to adults we tend to lose that wonder and begin to see just another lizard, horse, dog, elephant, or bird. We quickly forget that every life is precious, and we assume a misguided posture of superiority that renders other life forms inferior. This attitude conflicts with a deep appreciation for the earth grounded on the sacredness of all life and celebration of its existence.

Colin Fletcher experienced an appropriate sense of awe during a rafting trip down the mighty Colorado River. He was reflecting on the beauty of billion-year-old red sandstone when a cloud of mayflies distracted his contemplation: "Backlit by sunbeams, diaphanous body and extended whisks stood out in startling relief against the shadowed rock wall. And in each such interval of slow descent the dancer attained a peak of grace and beauty. . . ." If placed in the same spot at the same time, most of us would never have even noticed these insects living out their brief existence. They would only be background noise.

Fletcher goes on to observe the juxtaposition of an insect versus a human compared to the sandstone cliff looming stoically for one billion years. He ponders: "But against the time scale of the background rock, was there really much difference between twenty-four hours and three score and ten? Was there any difference at all?" Here is the heart of the matter. A deep connection with the earth recognizes that in the grand scheme of things all life, not just human life, is to be revered. In terms of actual length, our own existence is virtually insignificant. We share this fact with all other living things. Therefore, we should celebrate all living things.

Unfortunately, in modern life a disconnect occurs between making a living and living a life. This disconnect places greater emphasis on the means of living—economic gain—than on the ends, namely, living a full life. As a result, we tend to depreciate the sacredness of our lives and those of others inhabiting this earth. This in turn creates insulation from nature and reinforces a culture that does not value the wild earth.

In his book *Halflives*, Brooke Williams explores the intriguing idea of the disconformity between wilderness and work. He reflects on the difficulty of reconciling the two, a plight characterizing the curse of modern life. Heart and spirit cry to pursue physical activity, replenishment of soul, and camaraderie with friends when sharing enjoyable moments in nature. However, there is always a sword hanging over our heads: the responsibilities of personal and professional life. A job must be honored because it enables other achievements for happiness in life. But, slowly, work and personal relations begin to erode that carefree spontaneity and link to the wild world.

Little by little, the fun things in life and the very sacredness of life are traded off for a little more—a little more pay, a little higher authority and respect, a little better position from which to launch the next professional move, and a little better opportunity for retirement security. As these trade-offs are increasingly made, we begin to recognize that the sum is adding up. We have a lot less life left to live, a lot less physical capacity to do the fun stuff, and a lot less flexibility to run off and play when conditions scream for us to do otherwise.

The really bold ones just chuck it all and go for it. The rest wonder what it must be like. The mass of us live lives of anguished desperation and grieve over the hike not taken, the river not rafted, and the slope left unskied. Meanwhile, we contemplate the time when we will have to answer whether the sacrifices were worth the cost.

One Monday morning, I decided to take advantage of a fine spring day by hiking up the east side of the Sandia Mountains to Cienega Pass. It was a beautiful morning, with a latent crispness in the early morning but a strength in the sun that foretold the coming intensity of summer.

Aspens, willows, and black locust had recently emerged at the trailhead. Their shockingly fluorescent green leaves would harden over the next weeks in preparation for the long, hot summer. The world was brimming full of life, with insects in the air and birds calling and defending their territories: "Look at me. My feathers are brighter. I am bigger. I can fly faster." That's the great thing about stealing a weekday for oneself. Everyone is gone, and the forest springs back to life. Animals have the ability to know, or at least sense, that the weekend is over, and that they now have greater range for undetected movement. The forest is vibrant with their presence. Each turn in the trail offers the possibility of an unexpected surprise.

Cienega Spring was flowing flush with clear cool water, pushing fresh gallons from the depths of the earth. Waters wove a merry path alongside the trail dropping into travertine terraces and mini-waterfalls. The forest canopy arched overhead, dampening sounds and providing shade. Yellow rays of early light slanted through the trees to illuminate the gracefully flowing waters, unhurried in their passage. Over fallen limbs and encrusted stones it rolled down the mountainside. Light sparkled as the stream rose and fell over and around these temporary obstacles.

The Cienega Trail rises up very steeply in climbing three hundred feet. The term "trail" does not quite capture the steep ascent over roots and rocks, almost akin to climbing a ladder. A challenge is to finish this stretch without stopping to catch your breath. The last eighty feet are over sharp rocks seemingly determined to make certain that you do indeed stop. The trail then levels off into a spruce, aspen, oak, and pine forest that has been transformed over the last ten years by a heavy infestation of voracious bugs that has left gaping holes in the canopy. New spruce and fir are springing up with the generous sunlight, but it will be many years before the forest returns to its former health.

Squirrels chided me as I climbed upward. Spruce trees that had survived the bug devastation offered some sustenance to the tassel-eared giants. It was obviously not the weekend, since squirrels tend to be reclusive when hordes of people are around. Their chatter presented a good diversion, as the trail grew steep climbing past large ponderosa with red cinnamon bark and rehabilitating spruce that once again could send forth an optimistic flourish of needles. Greater moisture at this elevation results in an abundance of deep green grass and flowers along the trailside, and with it a greater prevalence of life.

The path picked its way over rocks and roots in an unrelenting climb toward the crest. I was lost in thought about a new assignment at work and the realization that I was making the trade-off Brooke Williams lamented—work for passion. My time would not be my own. Did I really want to do this? The new assignment would provide plenty of opportunities to touch the lives of others in meaningful ways, but my love for the outdoors would suffer. This sacrifice was now becoming very real, and I went to the woods to reaffirm my belief in and commitment to the sacredness of life and wild things.

Two

Sun filtered down through the leaves, shedding brightness on my otherwise dreary mood. I was surrounded by the rich smell of moist earth; the startling freshness of clean air; the silence of the forest; the beauty of old trees that have stood the test of time and that show their wounds for the effort; the optimistic ascent of this year's flowers and grasses that would nourish wildlife; the mix of warm and chill as the sun played on the tree tops and barren areas; and, the sense of place, or home, known for many years.

The steep climb leveled out in a drainage flowing down from the crest. The lushness of this ravine is remarkable, with pines giving way to aspens and spruce. It leaves the impression that you have been transported several hundred miles north. The tread was damp and in places slightly muddy. A bucolic scene reflected an infinite pastel of green: bright green oaks, dark blue-green spruces, brilliant green aspens, and deep green yarrow.

This ravine terminated at the crest after a series of steep switchbacks and krumholz oak. Gnarly oak hovered over the trail, while younger, low-lying shrubs presented an impenetrable mass. I could see outcroppings of white-yellow limestone rock forming the crest just one hundred feet higher. It had been a great morning, even though I had not resolved that tension between wildness and work.

Upward the switchbacks climbed, as the trail grew steeper. Lush grasses, still damp with dew, caressed my legs as I passed. About to exit the krumholz and enter onto rock capping the crest, the path would open to sun and breeze coming from the pass to the west.

Turning the final switchback, I heard lots of noise and commotion in the oaks to my right. A herd of deer was often drawn to this lush ravine, and they must have sensed my presence. It was very likely that I would run into them on a Monday. They could take the risk of grazing at a busy trail intersection without the weekend's probability of seeing humans. I was embarrassed for intruding and tried to walk as quietly as I possibly could. They really deserved the week off. This was the time of plenty. Let them enjoy their happiness. Let them enjoy the fat of the land. Let them enjoy the way it used to be without our noisy, threatening, and smelly intrusion into their lives. Let them raise their young confidently with the thought toward these green pastures.

On scattered rock I semi-scrambled the last distance to the crest. Through a dark copse of sheltered spruce, out of the wind, the way turned dark before opening among locust bushes. And then I heard a scramble through the oaks and locusts to the north about twenty yards away. These were either extremely clumsy or excessively large deer to make that much noise. I quickly walked several paces to a rock out-cropping and climbed up. There to the north was a magnificent brown bear in full form. She paused and looked back my way. Gad, she was beautiful. In the prime of the season and health, she must weigh close to three hundred pounds. Her head was huge. How can these bears grow this large in a land that is often struck by drought?

She lingered and gazed my way, but the commotion in the bushes did not stop. And then they emerged. Two very large cubs scooted ahead of her. These were not little cubs enjoying their first years. These were second-year cubs about to be fledged. They were enormous, and their size clearly spoke to a well-fed year last summer. Both mama and the cubs were a dark rich brown, with little variation in their fur. These were very healthy animals. They had caught my scent by a zephyr of wind when I was walking within a few feet of them down in the krumholz. That would explain the crashing through the underbrush.

Mother bear and cubs now fully recognized exactly what I was. They slowly began to climb a ridge north of me. There, amid the stunted blue spruce, gnarled oak, and profuse locust, the cubs picked their way up the ridge. The cubs paused about ten feet in front of their mother, and the three of them glanced back my way, sniffing the air. This is as wild as it gets, I thought. Bears full of life. A day of perfection. A classic encounter between bear and human, a visible reminder of the sacredness of life.

And then they were gone. They picked their way up the ridge and vanished to the north. Was it two hours that we had shared or two min-utes? It was difficult to say. As things returned to normal I longed for more—more interaction of the wild kind and a deeper drink from the sacredness of life. These few moments argued persuasively that life is too important to trade off wildness for material gain. I had been lucky to see the dance of life by these bears, and I still resonate with the thrill, the love of a wild earth.

Cognizant that I had received a rich and unexpected blessing, I turned and started my way home. Or was it away from home?

While the east side of the Sandia Mountains offers lush vegetation and a feeling that resembles Colorado, the west side is unlike any other place I know. Lower reaches start in high grass–dominated desert and wind their way up into heavier forest, forest that appears whenever there is the least bit of water or shade. Rocky crags of the west slope dominate the view of the Sandias for most of the metropolis at its feet. Rising a mile above Albuquerque, these mountains offer a varying complexion. Whether it is the pure white snow of winter, the harsh glaring sun of a full summer's day, or the subtle evening light that turns the Sandia Mountains watermelon red, thousands of people living at her base continually see a new face as the mountain watches over her domain. This west face is most frequented, since many trails are easily accessible within minutes from anywhere in Albuquerque. In twice the time that it takes to drive over to the east side, a strong walker can reach the crest from the west side.

I began the final four switchbacks toward the pass on Sandia Crest. The last half-mile begins on a sunny southern slope strewn with oak that warms you to the marrow after the climb through a spruce and aspen forest. Still, it gets cool above 8,500 feet, and four miles into the hike, I could sense the inevitable changes that come with altitude and the more forgiving slant of the sun's rays.

Only a little more than an hour earlier I had started in high-desert grasses, cholla cactus, Spanish bayonet, and a scattering of Rocky Mountain juniper with raucous blue jays squawking their dominance in staccato tones. The sun was just beginning to come up over the Sandia Mountains, and the air was decidedly brisk. Another day in the Land of Enchantment, where city folk would go about their business of soccer games, shopping, and life amid the scent of roasting chile and initial hint of color among the cottonwoods and willows. Only a fortunate few would venture toward the mountains.

The day was perfect. A warming sun counterbalanced the slight crispness to the air. The first fifteen minutes on the trail produced the typical thoughts and encounters. "Tighten up that shoulder strap. Too warm for gloves. Not yet time to remove the long-sleeve shirt. Lots of birds out this morning. No mountain bikers out this morning. Colors are really starting to show on the oaks."

Once the trail entered the designated wilderness, a slow predictable trudge began, and with it a gradual change in the wilderness. High desert gave way to low mountain forest. Live oaks and bushy junipers dominated a landscape that increasingly saw an occasional piñon and a multitude of mountain mahogany. The terrain changed from the gentle slope of an alluvial plain to true mountain hill and ridge. Decomposed granite formed the base with large boulders cast upon the forest floor.

The trail entered its toughest phase—a ramble up one minor ridge and down into a wash; up another incline and down into a wash. All the time the path weaved in and out of the boulders and copses of Gambel oak. What a beautiful mix of plant life, rock, and sky. Enough space for thoughts to wander freely. Enough light to bathe in without suffering the grief of excessive heat. Enough peace to repair your soul. Lots of verbal displays by many birds this morning, which remained hidden among the branches and leaves.

A slow amble over hill and dale changed suddenly as ponderosa pines became plentiful among the piñon and oak. Mountain mahogany began to recede among vegetation that thrived on slightly greater moisture and coolness and slightly less light. The gradient of the trail rose sharply through Apache plume, chamisa, and Mormon tea in and around the washes.

I entered the realm of gnarly ponderosa pines. Many decades ago a heavy snowfall must have hit this particular glade where ponderosa pines had taken a stand against the elements, and the trees were twisted into curlicues. The trail entered a quiet bowl dominated by the towering trees where the ground is covered by a rich duff of needles and debris, adding to the cathedral-like feel. The forest canopy was now dense and the air chilled by the giants within the grove.

I thought back to a similar walk with friends two years ago at this same time of the year. We descended quickly into the bowl without carrying on much conversation. There in the middle of the bowl was a small black bear that sprinted for cover. This was one of those split-second sightings that doesn't offer much in the way of visualizations, but sets your heart racing nonetheless. One second I was absorbed in the climb and socializing, and the next bewildered by the frantic crashing of a black streak with an enormous rear end. In the years since I saw that sight, I have taken to walking a bit softer, being a bit quieter, and scanning the forest and brush for another glimpse of the bear.

On exiting this bowl, the trail becomes more mountainous. The canopy continues to provide luxuriant shade and the forest takes on a hush while the trail itself loses its decomposed granite base and is replaced by dirt and forest duff. Ridges are more open to sun, and the trail alternates between spruce and pine glens to oak and ponderosa pine openings. The way grows distinctly steep and presents occasional views to the mountain crest. Looking to the west, you can mark progress not only in gaining altitude, but also in leaving the city behind. You are surrounded by mountains, bathed in them. Rock spires of the upper mountain loom to the north. All the while the temperature has continued to moderate. The morning chill is being lost to the sun's reverie at the same time that the growing altitude replenishes the sense of being cold. In the deep recesses and folds of the mountain the air is very cool and signals what awaits at the western, shady side of the crest.

Squirrels are dropping spruce cones like bombs onto the trail. Passing a couple of seeps that have ignored the drought, now through aspens and spruce, I find a perennial spring with a modest flow of water. This is where the trail becomes most pleasing, alive with the sound of hermit thrushes singing their fabulous trilling melody. It continues to climb steeply through two ravines and around one ridge. What a tempting detour the ravines with their shady delights, trickling water, and aspen-filled depths offer to travelers.

Ahead is a stand of brilliant aspen nearing its peak color. How gorgeous. The trees are solid yellows with no orange or red—just eye-catching batons of yellow flame amid a sea of green. A cobalt blue sky sets the finest backdrop to these trees. It is a magical moment and a time of grace.

The trail enters shade and grows steep. Over a downed tree; across several small boulders that focus your attention; across a stump, and toward the end of the first switchback in this final ascent to the crest. The glow of exercise and sense of accomplishment are intermingled with the deep sense of peace in a hallowed enclave of the forest. The mountain gives all she can give to a person: an extraordinary mixture of beauty; cool air from the previous night blending with the warming morning; the rich dank smell of moist earth overlaid with the slight hint of fall decay from summer's end; and, a distinct sense of life—the mountain as a living, breathing organism.

Rounding a curve and entering a vale where aspens stand, I looked up into the ethereal golden glow of the trees. For that brief moment I was allowed to transcend beyond humanness and to savor the sacredness of life. I felt the spirit of the mountain in my very heart and soul.

Past the aspens, I continued upward through oaks that were surrendering to the season with mottled brown leaves. Only a few more days and this moment of exquisite beauty would be a memory. The gentle breeze coming over the pass was chilly, but I was a switchback away and nearing the finale quickly. At the crest, sun claimed the open, low-growing vegetation. But the brisk breeze whisked its warmth away. No other hikers were at the pass. I stopped, took a swig of water, put on my hat and a long-sleeve shirt, and headed back down.

Still high on the mountain, I came to a favorite glade where water gathers as a constant tiny stream. You can hear its almost impercepti- ble trickle—the sound and music of mountain water. At the top of the valley was a couple with their dogs taking a break. "Hi. How are you doing today?" I asked. "Just fine," they replied. The dogs would not even look my way. They gazed off to the west from where they had come. I continued down the trail, thinking that a dog would provide a strong measure of companionship and debating the merits in my mind.

The trail skirted high above the deepening vee-shaped glade. Water trickled forty feet below. Sometimes it was visible and louder; in other places it was invisible and muffled. Here the aspens were still green and their exquisite white bark provided a counterpoint to the green of spruces and firs. Despite a hard, dry summer, they proclaimed an opti- mism that drought could never conquer. Then brush began breaking down by the stream. I saw movement but could not determine what was making the commotion. No question but that it was big. A few more steps down the trail might improve the view, and then, like so many situations before, time began to slow to a crawl.

I went about five paces and looked beyond the aspen and scatter- ing of shrubs to the stream itself, glistening in the rays of bright sun penetrating the canopy. At that moment a large dark brown bear crossed the creek in a single stride and headed north into the brush up the mountainside. This was an impressive bear, obviously drawn to the water and lush vegetation. She did not look in my direction as her shaggy head was going somewhere in a big hurry and with a distinct purpose. There was barely time to marvel at her thick, dark brown fur glistening in that moment of sun. More branches were breaking. And there they came. The first cub was almost black, but with tinges of brown. It jumped across the stream and lunged toward its mother. On the other side of the stream, it paused to look back—at me? No, to ascertain where its sibling was in this escalating dash. And here came the second cub. A light brown fuzz ball with legs. It too scampered up the hillside after plunging over a silvered fallen aspen blocking its path.

The last cub broke free of the entanglement presented by the fallen aspen and scooted up the hill. I began to breathe again, with thoughts toward the size of the cubs. They were pretty small for this late in the season. They could not have been much more than fifty or sixty pounds. This did not seem very large to me, not that they would lack from any protection by a mother that size. Would they make it through the winter?

I hurried on down the trail, more floating than walking. What a day this had been. The normal marvels—the trees, rocks, and microclimates—were just as wonderful going downhill as when going up. But now they seemed even more important. They contained the ingredients that allowed those bears to live and thrive. A world full of life. And for a brief moment I was part of this beautiful scene, a scene that was as old as time itself.

Two days later I broke free from work to repeat the walk, but not this time to achieve the crest. I wanted to return something to the bears. So, very early one morning my pack was loaded with a fresh bag of apples—an offering of thanks for the bears, and for the rest of the animals in this forest. The apples weighed me down, but I rationalized that it was helping me to keep in shape.

Up through the different climatic zones and vegetation I went until arriving at the spot where the encounter occurred. I then walked off trail for a few hundred yards because I did not want these bears, or any other animal, associating food with humans. I also wanted to prevent any bear-person encounter. There on a very steep hillside I offered to whichever animals would partake Red Delicious apples from a farm up near Bandelier National Monument. Perhaps these gifts would make a difference in the lives of the bears or other animals that frequented this garden. Spreading them on the ground, I backed away and hoped for the best.

That next weekend I returned to the crest. The day was warm and overcast. Little did I know that this cloud cover was the harbinger of things to come for several weeks. The weather was changing and would soon become cold and wet.

Racing up the trail, occasionally thinking about my previous encounter a week earlier, I reached the site and went over to check on the apples. They had all been consumed, but I couldn't make out any sign. Back on the trail I continued upward with a smile. I felt good about what I did, fully aware that it was an offense as far as the "authorities" are concerned. To them a fed bear is a dead bear.

Spirits in the Sandias

On entering the upper end of the trail and the last switchbacks, in the south-facing opening of the forest I gazed up to another stand of aspen, the last at peak color. Yellow leaves stood in sharp contrast to the azure sky, becoming hazy and cloud-strewn. These trees were at the lowest elevation on the north face of the mountain and thus had taken extra time to turn.

I plodded onward to the crest. On top, and now directly in the sun, a stiff, cold breeze was blowing. The last hundred feet of altitude gain and exposure to the winds had changed the conditions significantly. I pulled on long pants, a hat, and an extra shirt—time to get going in order to keep my warmth up. I dropped down the trail quickly in an effort to stoke the internal fire. Rounding the first switchback and looking straight ahead, I came across a good-sized mule deer in the middle of the trail. She was standing completely still with her giant ears trying to detect my sound. Her nose was twitching, working overtime to ascertain just what that figure was ahead. Friend or foe? She stood stock-still. I reassured her with gentle conversation and a slow approach. She angled off into the trees.

I walked quietly down the trail another fifty feet in an effort to see her, but she was gone. In another forty feet I reached the next switchback and turned the corner to see the rest of her companions. Five more deer, all does and yearlings, moved silently into the woods. How gracefully they walked. These woods were alive. The mountain opened her arms and embraced us.

These tales about encounters with bears, deer, and other wildlife in the Sandia Mountains suggest that the world is brimming with life. We have only to visit wild places to be blessed by this abundance of life. On these sojourns, we should be prepared for unexpected surprises that help us start down the path toward developing a love for the earth.

My adventures happened within close proximity of 750,000 people. This population becomes more aware of wildlife in the Sandia Mountains in late July, when bears begin invading backyards looking for food. Drawn by the aromatic smell of rotting fruit and driven by hunger to the land they once considered their own, but now controlled by humans, the bears seek ancient pathways to nourishment. In less urban times they were able to migrate freely down to the Rio Grande and its seasonal food supplies.

Most people do not see the bears' dance of life; they only harbor a sense of danger from wild animals. Having long ago traded off a close personal relationship with nature for material gain and urban comfort, they view bear invasions as a threat rather than a blessing or a natural expectation. Sadly, the love of material and worldly things has virtually extinguished their love for the earth.

Is it any wonder, therefore, that our society treats cats, dogs, and other pets as expendable commodities? If we had not lost perspective about nature and our love for the earth, our actions might be dramatically different. Would we continue to warehouse animals in prisons known as zoos? Wouldn't our society invest more resources in setting aside vast parcels of land to ensure the continuation of endangered species and to mitigate the need for zoos in the first place? Some conservationists see our national forests and parks as zoos because the scale of wild land set aside is simply insufficient to provide ecosystem integrity. They argue that wilderness land preservation must be greatly increased.

If every person adopted the view that we are no more important than that kitten abandoned in the alley, or that dog left day after day chained in the backyard with no companionship, the world would make more progress toward achieving an intelligent love for nature and the earth. As Gandhi said, we can judge the quality of a culture by the manner in which it treats animals.

In the end, our society faces a very difficult challenge in creating a nature-based culture. We should not let a difficult challenge become an impossible one, but it will take creative thinking. For example, the Wonderful Outdoor World Program helps city youth experience the wild by camping out in city parks and observing the stars at night. Teachers and other educators plant a seed about the fantastic world of nature. For many youth participating in the program, this is their first opportunity to see the possibilities of wildness.

The rest of us can also work on developing a deep love for the earth. We can commit to taking a walk every other day in a wild place or on an undeveloped parcel of land. Volunteer to improve a nature-based endeavor such as a bird sanctuary, wildlife center, or park. Support an earth-friendly nonprofit organization. Let your consumption vote for the environment. There are so many good options available to us all. We just need to get out of the box of urban thinking and back to a celebration of the sacredness of life.

3
Joy in the Bosque

The glowing yellow pastel light of a very early sunrise gradually filled the canyon arroyo with the promise of another clear, hot day. The sweet smell of morning wafting down from the mountainside momentarily argued that the day would not be a desiccating scorcher like the preceding days of hell. This heat wave would break soon, but not soon enough. Slowly clawing my way up the steep trail out of the canyon, I left the cool damp air behind. Bouncing over decomposing granite boulders, brushing aside the intruding four-wing saltbush, Apache plume, grasses, and mountain mahogany, and slipping on the gravely trail, I hurried to finish the walk while the coolness lasted.

As I came to the end of a short switchback amid piñon, boulders, and oak, the sounds of scurrying feet and quick movements through the brush surrounded me. What was going on? Down to the right about ten feet was a little fox struggling to climb through the maze of rocks and bush limbs. The parents were above me by about six feet. They were none too happy and communicated this with all the aggressive vigor they could muster. Their barking was no idle threat, and it quickly became apparent that I needed to get out from between them and the kit. With a few strides the problem was resolved to my satisfaction, but not theirs. They barked and snarled at me for another five minutes while I made my way up the hillside, and then they faded, slowly, silently, into the forest.

The fox family had ventured down to the stream for a last drink before the day began. My timing was lousy in terms of disturbing them, but perfect in confirming the unexpected bounty of life in this canyon and desert forest. Just yesterday I took this same trail and came upon the tracks of a big bobcat in the snow. I wanted to convince myself that the prints were those of a mountain lion, for with enough ungodly early morning rambles, even the stealthiest lion will be detected in time.

It is difficult, if not impossible, to walk in a forest, around a lake, alongside the ocean, or through a meadow without detecting the vibrant presence of life. But what we do with this knowledge or how we act after recognizing this glorious fact is another thing entirely. Most people simply blend back into the materialistic fabric of urban life having had a touch-ing experience that did not penetrate their consciousness. They did not truly register the presence and value of a world brimming with life.

A culture that loves wildness is cognizant of the prevalence of life and acts to protect and steward this special gift. In *The Abstract Wild*, Jack Turner conveys this commitment to the sacredness of life:

> I am on the side of the grizzly sow and her two cubs in the south fork of Snowshoe Canyon; the mountain lion who tracked my favorite Escalante hollow; the raven cooing at me while I shave on my porch; the ticks that cling to me each spring when I climb Blacktail Butte; the Glover's silk moth fighting the window pane; the pack rat that lives in my sleeping cave on the saddle between the Grand and Middle Tetons and scurries across my sleeping bag at night; the wind roaring in the mountains; the persistent virus that knocked me down this winter; the crystalline light that greets me when I step outdoors; the starry night.

Turner goes on to express the exceptionally important idea that we should uplift this abundant life gift from nature. Our society needs more people who maintain this love for the earth and who see wildness as compatible with modern life.

Teeming with life, the wetlands of the Bosque del Apache spread before us, glistening in the mellow sunlight of that December afternoon. Our senses were filled to the brim and beyond. Birdcalls owned the air—honk-ing, cawing, tremolos, screeches, squawking, quacking, and every imagi-nable bird vocalization known to the human ear. Visits to this forest along the Rio Grande a couple of hours' drive south of Albuquerque mark the high point of each year. This is a time to regenerate with the wonder of life and to reaffirm a commitment to let more of nature into your life, and to let more of the material world out. It is impossible to walk among the flocks without somehow recognizing that another whole world of nature exists out there from which people are detached and isolated. Some will slowly realize that without this world they have already died a little death.

He drove the van so proudly down Interstate 25 toward the little town of Socorro. Bill had purchased a new van. It was a bulbous sort of vehicle, wide, squat, and short—not the type of car that would be easy to negotiate through city traffic or mall parking lots. The van rode high, and the wide expanse of the front windshield helped to bring the vastness of the New Mexico landscape into the car.

Bill suggested that we drive to the bosque that early Sunday afternoon to "see the birds." Having never been to the bosque before, I had no understanding of what this might bring. And so, on that bright December day, with few clouds and modest wind but temperatures in the very low forties, we launched the land yacht toward the south and began the journey. Leaving Albuquerque at 1:00 in the afternoon, we were all prepared with binoculars, mittens, coats, and drinks, settling back to the rhythm of the road and a cleansing from city life.

Within five miles of leaving the city limits, there are vivid reminders of how Albuquerque sits as an isolated island among the vastness of the high desert. Homes soon petered out as the high grasslands and scrub-filled arroyos dominated. But along the Rio Grande an entirely different microclimate embraces the river. The bosque is full of high cottonwood trees, willows, and other vegetation dependent on the river for its nourishment. This green swath extends nearly a mile on each side of the riverbank as it announces the presence of water in the otherwise arid landscape of the high desert.

The bosque was once made rich not only by water, but also by a periodic replenishment of nutrients and fresh soil in floods that regularly swept the river channel. It counted on this resurrection, whether from high snows or flash flooding from the sometimes-torrential monsoon rains in summer. All of this has been tamed by our dams that control flooding and thus safeguard the value of the land. Of course, we failed to recognize that by controlling the floods, the wildness of the river and the replenishment of soil and habitat would also be destroyed.

The introduction of nonnative plants such as the salt cedar or tamarisk further degraded the bosque. This invasive interloper sucks up vast quantities of water and dominates the natural vegetation. Along with Russian olive, the salt cedar has remade the riparian environment so that stately cottonwoods cannot regenerate. The nonnative forest attracts abundant wildlife such as migrating birds, but the precise impact on the ecosystem is not clear.

We sped toward Socorro. The Sevilleta Game Refuge soon appeared. These wild lands are formed from side branches and backwaters of the Rio Grande. Flocks of white snow geese floated in the shallow murky water among brush and bushes. Indeed, congregations of sandhill cranes were foraging among the fields, and swarms of snow geese pecked at the stubble looking for food. In the sky above the refuges and the Rio Grande, bands of cranes, snow geese, and Canadian geese were flying along in formation.

Twenty minutes south of Socorro, the Bosque del Apache appeared amid towering cottonwoods and willows. Almost thirteen thousand acres form the core of the preserve along the Rio Grande with additional acreage outside the wetlands. Approximately four thousand acres are within the Rio Grande floodplain. The refuge includes a visitor's center and assorted support buildings, but the center of the action is a fifteen-mile tour loop on dirt roads.

In the final miles approaching the refuge, flocks of birds were everywhere—ground, air, trees, and fields. Within the refuge, life exploded around us. I have never seen so many birds in one place, with innumerable varieties, including ducks, swans, eagles, hawks, coots, egrets, geese of several types, shorebirds, pelicans, terns, and cranes.

The more charismatic birds, such as whooping cranes and eagles, drew passionate attention and admiration among visitors on the viewing stands. Golden and bald eagles perched in dead trees amid the vast rectangular ponds. At the fringes of the ponds stood huge cottonwood trees that also served as convenient perches for eagles and various hawks. Wind rippled the shallow murky waters of the ponds where clumps of brown grasses from the previous summer poked up like islands. Birds darted everywhere and the noise was raucous. The surrounding mountains might be hibernating with the winter snow, but here was easily accessible nature of the best type.

The rectangular fields are roughly half a mile wide and a mile long. Some were filled with shallow water, while others were left dry, thanks to a rotation plan established for the refuge. Birds fed in all spots. Canals delivering water to the fields bordered the dirt road and offered a rich habitat for lush vegetation. Shrubs along these banks provided shelter for smaller birds that flitted in and out of the leafy safety zones. In the fields, larger birds flocked. A constant, soothing burble of birdcalls hung over the refuge. In the waning sun this sacredness of the bounty of life was hard to miss. The birds had traveled many miles to reach this haven for the winter. But even here they could not relax because of lurking predators like coyotes, eagles, and hawks.

Joy in the Bosque

To the east, in the tall grasses of a field, a pheasant with brilliant feathers sought shelter while the iridescent green of its neck glinted in the sun. A bit farther along were several deer browsing in the shrubbery. We pulled up to another lookout and gazed upon hundreds of white snow geese standing in a dry field. Their constant chatter was inspiring. Some slept. Some ate. Some fought. Meanwhile, floods of geese were constantly arriving from the north with the waning day.

At the northern loop the number of vans, sedans, and SUVs concentrated along the fields increased noticeably. The grain in these fields must be superior in abundance or quality, judging by the number of birds that congregated in the five-foot-high stubble and along the mown edges. They clearly voted this northern end as the spot of choice.

We watched as a coyote, off in the distance, made a dash for a snow goose along a ridge separating the fields. The goose escaped just in time, and the coyote sauntered along at a lope looking for easier pickings. He quickly vanished into the brown rows of seed stalks. It was apparent why most of the birds remained on the edge of the fields, but bolder members hunted within the stalks for morsels. Cranes were most brazen, walking in their stiff, stilted way while vocalizing constantly.

Folks with binoculars glued to their faces scanned the flocks, while others brandished high-power and high-dollar spotting scopes. Whooping cranes were sighted among a flock of about one hundred cranes, the giveaway being their distinctive white plumage compared to the dull gray of the sandhill cranes. Excitement flowed throughout the crowd. For a moment everyone seemed to forget the increasing chill and the gathering darkness. With great exuberance, people shared in a reverent way about the whooping cranes. For a brief eternity these visitors were drawn together by an uncommon experience. Formations of inbound birds from the purple haze of night to the north were rapidly arriving at the far edge of the fields. At 4:30 p.m., with the sun making its final appearance, a spectacular phenomenon unfolded. As if on cue, the snow geese lifted off simultaneously from the fields and joined their incoming comrades for a massive community fly. There were thousands upon thousands of snow geese flying overhead everywhere. They churned as if stirred by an unseen wooden spoon. Often flying no more than thirty feet off the ground, birds darted around at all sorts of elevations. The honking was deafening.

Three

This spectacle continued for about ten minutes and birds swirled everywhere. You could almost feel yourself caught up with the flocks as they shouted their joy, exclaiming their good fortune in surviving the rigors of flying up and down the Rio Grande in search of food. They celebrated the simple joy of being snow geese. And then, as quickly as it began, the birds settled down onto the fields and into tight white clumps like ungathered cotton as they prepared to spend the night.

On our way out of the refuge, in the dying light, surprises continued to materialize. Here was a large goshawk. There was a slender egret in the marsh. Here were platoons of ducks nibbling away on aquatic vegetation. There was a golden eagle in a cottonwood tree almost unrecognizable in the growing darkness. How fulfilling such a simple experience this was. In a refuge brimming with life, each visitor took away a vibrant memory of a special day and communion with the birds.

Repeated visits to the Bosque del Apache became a benchmark to measure the quality of a year. The more visits to the bosque, the higher the quality of life. The joyous evening communal flights just before final sunset are a special attraction; consequently trips were scheduled to coincide with the birds' return from foraging. But there is always something new to see in this refuge, which is the personification of life. Some visits bring richer gifts than others; however, I never leave disappointed.

On a business trip to Las Cruces one February, I loaded my Eagle Optics binoculars with the idea of stopping at the bosque. I pulled up to the entrance at 2:00 in the middle of a warming afternoon. Few visitors were out at this hour, and the whole visit seemed pointless, since I had arrived at one of the worst times of the day for birding. Most birds would be gradually feeding at long distances up or down the Rio Grande. Nonetheless, since I was in the vicinity it was worth a look.

A golden eagle was the first bird spotted as it loomed in a dead tree. Dashing in front of the car, a sparrow hawk chased a hapless bird through the bushes. Several species of ducks bobbed gently on rolling currents of the lakes. There is nothing quite like going back to a favorite wild area, and it felt good to be home again. The visit confirmed that most of the larger birds—geese and cranes—had left the refuge for better foraging along the fields and among the farms radiating from the bosque. Nonetheless, there was plenty of wildness to see and savor.

As I approached the north end of the loop road, I saw a small group of snow geese huddled in the middle of a low-cut field. Their pure white feathers contrasted sharply with the brown stubble. I opened the door and stepped out into the warm sunshine and still air. There was nary a soul around. Stretching felt good after the long drive, and I glassed toward a distance group of snow geese and sandhill cranes. Incredibly, there in the far corner of the northern field was a whooping crane. I gazed for a long while at the beautiful bird, knowing that its number is diminishing at the refuge. I slipped back behind the steering wheel and turned the first corner of the loop. A coyote sauntered across the road.

At home I searched the Internet for the bosque's home page to keep track of the bird count. With some finagling and detective work, the site eventually surfaced. Sorting through the menu, I found a cryptic note that primitive camping is available on a reservation basis to educational and volunteer groups. It sounded like a fantastic opportunity to spend the night with the birds.

Days turned into months and the seasons passed. Soon it was late fall again, and the thought of squeezing in one more camping trip sounded good. The bosque immediately came to mind, so I pulled out the old computer-generated file and checked it against the latest posted information at the site before calling to ascertain specifics on the reserved camping. A volunteer assistant informed me that there were two large group campgrounds without water, but with outhouses and fire pits available for reservation. I requested a site for the day after Thanksgiving.

In the following days, summer turned into winter. Day after day of snow and rain pelted New Mexico, and the temperature plummeted. Fortunately, my friend Don and his son Ralph saved me. Don had not been to the bosque in some time. The Thanksgiving break gave him time off from work, and fortunately Ralph would be visiting and was eager to go along.

It snowed five inches in the three days prior to our reservation, and temperatures were very low for this time of year. Daytime highs were in the low forties and night temperatures were in the low twenties to teens. In view of the fact that the bosque is along the Rio Grande, it would be that much colder due to the moisture and the tendency for cold air to sink.

At noon Don gave me a call. I was certain that he was calling to cancel, but fortunately he was all set to go. "We will need tons of wood, Don. Are you certain that we have enough?" "Sure, but we do need white gas for the stove. Can you bring some along?" I loaded up extra wood in my car as well as white gas and headed to Don's house.

I claimed the back seat so that I could sleep on the way down. Already drowsy, the warm sun on the west side of the car began to take effect. The gentle rocking of the car had me falling asleep in seconds, only to be pulled back to the present by the conversation. After half an hour, the conversation quieted down and I began to dream of the coyotes that are persistently present in the bosque. With heavy eyes and nodding head, I thought back to many encounters with coyotes.

It had been an extremely difficult week. I returned home from a trip to San Diego to find my cat, Joy, slinking along the floor with eyes fully dilated. We rushed her to the veterinary hospital, where the vet immediately admitted her and began diagnostic tests. Initial x-rays indicated no major organ damage. The vet placed her on intravenous fluids and observation. The report the next day was not good. She had gone into consistent seizures and spasms. More tests were ordered, which provided little additional information. After the third night it was beginning to look grim.

During visitation, with a blanket for the hospital floor and many types of her favorite food, I hoped for the best. What a shock when she was brought into the room. Joy was a matted mess and could only stumble about the room. It was a pitiful sight. But she ate a bit of food. The vet was encouraged and felt that a spinal tap was the next invasive procedure needed. There really was little choice because the poor cat was still having seizures, but the spinal tap provided almost no new information. The vet reasoned that she might have had a stroke or hit her head. We discussed putting her down.

By repeated visits each day and spoon-feeding with some grooming, Joy began to improve slightly. The vet discharged her in hopes that her recuperation would continue. I called on a friend's father, who was also a vet, for a second opinion. He spent much time looking Joy over, asking questions and examining her before deciding that she either had suffered head trauma or had gotten into some poison. He recommended Prednisone in order to reduce swelling and to stimulate liver function. In twenty-four hours the difference in her condition was remarkable. His bill for $42.00 stood in stark contrast to the $1,987.00 tallied up by the scientifically driven veterinarian hospital.

Joy in the Bosque

Early that Sunday morning, I went out to get the paper, and Joy came along. She stopped at the garage while I went out to the end of the driveway. I stooped for a few seconds to tie my shoelace. When I looked back up Joy was gone. I was frantic. This was much too early for her to be outdoors in the foothills of Albuquerque. I ran around the house twice looking for her, to no avail. As I finished the second round, I looked up to see a neighbor walking his German shepherd. "Ah, that will chase the coyotes away if there are any," I thought to myself.

Entering my office off the garage, I left the door open and began to work. "Where is that damn cat?" I asked myself. That question was answered within the hour as I heard a distant commotion that drew me to the courtyard. Yes, there it was again, a kind of snarl mixed with the sound of a small dog barking. "Wait a minute," I told myself. "We don't have small dogs in this neighborhood, only big dogs." I located the noise in front of the neighbor's house and started toward it. Then things kicked into high gear, but they moved so slowly. It was as if time was standing still. Fifty yards away I could see the commotion of two animals. The thought burst through my brain, "Coyote."

I ran the fifty yards toward the scrambling animals and caught a glimpse of cat and coyote entangled. One last cat snarl and shriek and then I saw it. The coyote was headed for the street with Joy dangling from its mouth. The coyote had her head entirely in its mouth but Joy continued to struggle, raking the predator with her claws.

I intercepted the coyote just as it was about to set foot on the pavement. I knew that if the coyote reached the road, it would have that extra advantage and be gone, with Joy in its mouth.

I reached for the coyote's back. It turned to glance at me, spit Joy from its mouth, took three paces, and slowed to turn around. I scooped Joy up, a terrified mess. The coyote gave me a screw-you look, accelerated to the speed of light, and was gone. Joy had only a little blood from the coyote on her. She must have raked its snout with her claws, which probably accounted for the doglike yelp. The $2,000 cat was safe, and she would never again venture outside without me riding herd over her.

"Yes, what's that, Don?" I jerked back to reality as Ralph and Don asked about whether I would be joining them on a May hike in the Gila Wilderness. Little beads of perspiration were on my forehead. I had relived this memory more than once and it still captured my full attention. Having just passed Socorro, I sat alert ready to give directions for turning off the freeway.

We swung into the refuge exactly at 4:00 p.m. as the volunteer rangers closed up shop for the day. We asked about checking in for camping, and they said that the visitor's center was closed. "Just go on to the campground and set up. Thanks for telling us, as we would have wondered who was down there. No reason going up to the visitor center only to have to turn around and come back here." And with that we scooted through onto the loop to see birds.

A few patches of ice could be found in the small ponds in the middle of the loop, but otherwise the lake areas were not frozen. Birds flew everywhere—small birds, large birds, dark birds, light birds, birds of every shape and color. These initial minutes are a bit disconcerting when adjusting to all of that life swarming around you—life that most people simply take for granted. The first viewing stand was overflowing with people who were jockeying to see a golden eagle perched up in a tree. Like so many other times, the charismatic birds tend to attract crowds.

We came to the bend in the road that would take us up on the north loop with the entrance to the two group camps dead ahead. Ralph got out of the car and opened the gated barrier. Then Don drove the last mile down to the campsite in seclusion—what a great home this would be for the night.

The camp was on level, sandy ground with small cottonwood trees surrounding the area. Two metal fire pits surrounded three large picnic tables. Perfect! Within minutes we were headed back up the loop road to enjoy the final moments of the day. Pulling over by a small group of cars, we gazed upon two hundred snow geese honking and foraging in a field. Here and there were stately sandhill cranes strutting through the snow geese. The old familiar calls returned, and the dying rays of the sun warmed my cheeks as I glassed for the single whooping crane reported to be there in the bosque. The sacredness of life spread before us in hundreds of beautiful birds. Ralph pointed out eagles in nearby trees. In fact, many were actually larger hawks.

Back in the car, we drove the northern loop to another viewing stand and another large flock of snow geese—perhaps twice the size of the previous group. But now there were more sandhill cranes. The fine black edges on the wings of the snow geese were apparent when they stretched. Only a few Canadian geese were scattered here and there in little groups. We were impatient to get back to the northern end of the loop, where experience had taught that the most action occurred.

The north end of the bosque loop lived up to our expectations. We came upon a large group of cars off in the northeast corner. Several of the birdwatchers had massive professional spotting scopes. Over in a stand of cottonwoods were three bald eagles. They were enormous birds sitting up in the trees preening themselves and captivating the onlookers. After about ten minutes we pushed on for the top loop. The sun was setting, and the flocks were becoming active. Pulling over to the side of the dusty road, we found birds flying everywhere. We could see flocks coming down from the north in their vee formations. Honking and squawking, they landed with little grace among the growing throngs of those settled in for the night.

We stepped out of the car to a whirling mass of birds. I looked over at Don. He was just standing there with a grin on his face. He too sensed the deep enjoyment of this theater of life. We drank deeply in pleasure as something elemental touched our souls about the scene. It might have been our own spirits expressing thanks for a return to wildness. It was a moment of renewal and thanksgiving for the abundance of life.

We stopped one last time at the marsh where the smaller ducks tend to congregate. It was a wonderful last view of our feathered friends. Pulling on warmer clothes, we walked out on a viewing deck. A volunteer ranger was explaining things to people as birds flew in for the evening. "Look, here comes a sandhill crane. They have been out feeding in the fields all day long. The first thing they will do is dip down to take a long drink of water. There they go. They will now settle down for the night." Don edged over closer to the ranger to fill his insatiable curiosity. The ranger invited him to look through his spotting scope at a crane. It was going to be more difficult to get Don out of here than I thought.

At long last we retraced our route to the campground. Now quite dark, the task of setting up the tents was a challenge. Don backed the car by the fire pit and Ralph unloaded the firewood. I focused on trying to set up a tent in the semi-light given my frozen hands bundled in gloves.

Ralph is the world's expert in starting campfires, and he was putting his skill to great use while I pulled out the Coleman lantern. I had only used the lantern once and could not quite get it going fast enough for

Ralph. He took over and it popped to life—instant, brilliant light. The fire reached a steady blaze, and we crowded around the flames flickering upward into the night. It was only 5:00 p.m. I looked at the pile of firewood. Would it last?

Dinner unfolded quickly. There was no inefficient effort at this moment. Fortifying drinks suddenly appeared. Salsa and chips were opened and consumed with startling speed. Hamburger and seasoning went into the skillet. Tomatoes and bell pepper were diced and cheese grated. Huge flour tortillas were heated on the Coleman gas stove. Camp routine began to return. There around the blazing campfire we stuffed ourselves with the best burritos you could imagine. They always taste so much better when you are starved and cold like this. Life seemed pretty good at that moment. It had truly been worth all of the effort getting here.

Once dinner was done and the dishes washed, we settled down to the camaraderie of the campfire. I brought out several smudge sticks made from sage grown at home. The campsite and friends were bathed in the tangy scent of sage, a purification. We talked about many things. Ralph shared his experiences as a Peace Corps worker in Paraguay. Don talked about the Gila Wilderness and prospects for another year of fishing. Amid the flames and cigars we shared that crusty bread known as ourselves.

At 10:00 p.m. we let the coals die down and headed off to our beds. What a shock! The temperature had plummeted with the setting sun. Away from the fire, we spent some time gazing up at the stars. The almost utter void of light down at the bosque, and a moonless night had conspired to give us optimum stargazing. The Milky Way was so easily discernible. Planets were like suns. These moments tend to shake you to the very depths of your soul. With stars in our eyes, we drifted to our tents.

It was already well below freezing when we went to bed. Ice crystals were forming everywhere on the tent—this would be a very cold night. An hour later I had to get up. I stepped outside the tent and was greeted by a chorus of yips, howls, and wails from a pack of coyotes not more than thirty yards away. They sang a long melodious tune with many stanzas. They were very close.

I slept little this night. First I was too cold. Then I became too warm and had to remove most of my clothes. But what really prevented me from sleeping was the birds. There was a constant quacking, honking, and squawking. At intervals there would be a ruckus when a coyote came too near to the flock. They would become aroused and honk loudly. It was actually kind of funny to hear this all night. I did not anticipate getting much sleep and tried to enjoy the nearness of the flocks.

At 6:00 a.m. the sky began to lighten, I pulled on many layers and went for a short walk. What a great feeling. A new day was dawning. The ice was incredible—it was literally everywhere. Soon warm water led to hot chocolate and coffee. Even Don exited early, as he wanted to go see the birds. This was a tough choice—warm fire and breakfast or birds. We chose the birds.

We repeated our round on the loop. There were no new remarkable sights, yet we basked in a warm glow knowing that we did something special that no one else had done that night—we had slept among the birds.

The sun was just beginning to appear over the horizon, and as it sent the first rays of the day the birds all flew up into the air. They were flying everywhere—honking and celebrating the fact that a new day had dawned and that they were alive to greet it. Don just stood there with this grin on his face. "Can you believe it? Can you believe it?" He was aglow in the ebb and flow of life.

We once again made our way to the last viewing stand in the marsh. The same volunteer ranger was out holding court. The wooden structure was laden with half an inch of ice. No one complained about the ice or the cold. They were here to see birds and they were in their ecstasy.

Back in camp, I had planned just the right meal for this occasion. We quickly put on bacon, scrambled eggs, and potatoes O'Brien while water was heated for more hot chocolate and coffee. Ralph stoked the coals into a fire, and we had one of the very best camping breakfasts that I can remember. The poky old sun slowly climbed as we finished the warming meal. Yet, anything in shadow remained ice-rimed for quite some time. This was going to be a cold day.

In between sips of hot chocolate, I went over to the tent. It was raining in the center on my sleeping bags. The dome tent had that clever mesh skylight at the top for viewing stars. I had put on the rain fly in order to retain some heat. Now as the top of the rain fly warmed in the sun, condensation from the previous night fell.

After finishing breakfast and loading the vehicle, I think I noticed it first. There was a swirl of wind. I mentioned to Don and Ralph that we had been very lucky. If it had been windy last night, we would never have been able to stand around the campfire. It would have been one very long night. Then more gusts came up and soon we had a steady wind. The low must have been in the high teens last night, and with a significant wind chill, things were now turning ugly. Ralph put the fire out and jumped into the car.

We took one last swing around the loop. This was more of a gesture to say goodbye than anything else. As if to give us one last gift, several bucks crossed the loop road as we turned south. Two had fine antlers while a third had nubbins. We watched them grazing in the sun for a few minutes—an unexpected gift, but then that was what the bosque was all about. And with the heater going full bore, we ambled back home.

A culture that loves wildness will also uphold the sacredness of life. The Bosque del Apache is only one of thousands of governmentally administered sites where society gains access to a rich environment swarming with life. There are many other public and private venues that also offer opportunities to experience nature and its abundance. But even these venues are seldom necessary for intimate contact with wildlife that builds and reinforces our connection to the earth.

Eat your lunch outside today in a secluded spot, preferably under a tree. Relax and open yourself to nature. Feel the warmth of the sun or the chill of the breeze. Listen to the chirping of birds and the flutter of their wings as they soar about in their struggle for sustenance. Look down at the ants on the pavement or the beetle struggling with a morsel under your bench. Look closely at the spider web between the trashcan and the retaining wall. Are there more than just leaves caught in that web?

All of us can do a better job of embracing the earth every day of our lives. The effort required is minimal. By actively and passionately seeking to immerse ourselves in nature, we increase our chances to interact more with wild things, uphold the sacredness of life, and see wildness as compatible with modern civilization.

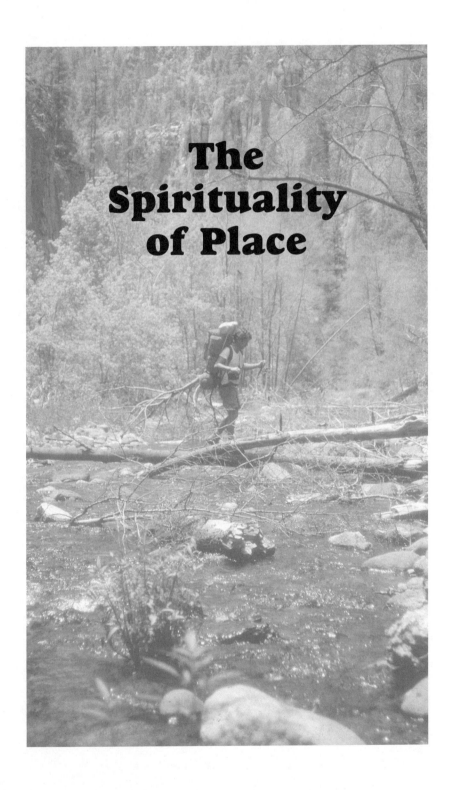

The Spirituality of Place

4
Bandelier National Monument

When I spend time spent in a flowered meadow strewn with wild purple iris and bordered by softly quaking aspen trees in the Pecos Wilderness or on a path deep within the cathedral canopy of hemlock and Douglas fir on the Olympic Peninsula, I inevitably reflect on the special qualities of wild places. Buffered from the intrusions of modern and urban life, and protected from the incessant media that fill our lives, it is easier to understand the wonderfully intangible personality of a meadow or forest cove. No two meadows or forests are alike. Each has distinguishing characteristics that set it apart and make it unique.

In her memoir *Begoso Cabin*, Mari Graña paints a vivid portrait of an abandoned sheepherder's stone cabin that she acquired on 240 acres of land in northern New Mexico. She relates, in exquisite detail, the special qualities of cabin, mesa, canyon, and creek that comprise her querencia. In the course of Graña's story we are led to understand that Begoso Cabin is more than a compilation of building and land. The specific ingredients—the cow pasture to the south of the cabin; the rutted and gullied dirt road lined with weathered juniper fence posts; the hovering hawks, magpies, and owls; the steep escarpment of the sage-filled mesa; cottonwoods in the arroyos; the nearby small community and its church—add to more than a sum of the separate parts. Graña poignantly describes the spirit reflected at Begoso Cabin.

The spirituality of place is vividly alive and recognizable throughout nature. A culture that embraces the earth will also cherish the unique spirits reflected in a mountain glade, an ocean cove, or a desert wash. Fortunately, there is a rich legacy of literature devoted to celebrating this spirituality of natural areas.

In *The Book of Yaak*, Rick Bass captures the wild spirit of the Yaak Valley in northwestern Montana with its virgin forests and charismatic animals—grizzlies, wolves, lynx, martens, and eagles. In *Living on the Spine*, Christina Nealson reflects on a mystical life in the Sangre de Cristo Mountains in southern Colorado, where starlight, piñon trees, mountain bluebirds, and a wandering black bear nourish a gentle earth spirit. Perhaps the seminal discourse on the spirit of place was *Walden* by Henry David Thoreau. In a semi-wild enclave of Massachusetts, Thoreau detailed a life embracing nature and the spirit of Walden Pond.

Remote wilderness rivers and mountains are not the only places on this earth that emanate spirituality. Granted, there is pervasive recognition of the power surrounding the Himalayas, the Sangre de Cristo Mountains looming over Santa Fe and Taos, the depths of the Grand Canyon, or the red rock country of Moab. However, we frequently find the spirit of place in more common, less wild, settings such as a small garlic farm in New Mexico that Stanley Crawford describes in *A Garlic Testament* or the small uplands farms of the Vermont hills John Elder celebrates in *Reading the Mountains of Home*.

In developing a deeper connection with the earth, our society would benefit significantly by seeking and uplifting the spirituality of place. By recognizing the spiritual characteristics of all places, we would then treat the land with greater respect and with diminished utilitarian insight. Ironically, we need to turn to precisely that which we know least in order to develop a culture that loves the earth. The answer is found in mountains, rivers, valleys, deserts, seashores, swamps, glaciers, and other natural areas that call to us.

On a wonderful mild October day with the sun trying to shine through a pastiche of cottony clouds, we headed toward Painted Cave in Bandelier National Monument. How memorable fall days can be. Chiles roasting within rotating propane-fired cylinders offer a nostalgic reminder of this most beautiful season in New Mexico. Days turn bathwater warm after very crisp nights. The long hot summer is broken. Fireplaces emit the sweet scent of piñon smoke as shop owners in Santa Fe and Old Town Albuquerque drive off the chill morning. Chamisa blooms with golden flowers expelling a melancholy scent—a smell evoking both pleasant memories and hope—hope for a new year, hope for dreams unfilled, and hope that the winter will bring magnificent moisture to the land in rain and snow.

Bill and Terrye chatted about something in the front seats of the car while I fell into a trance. A smug smile graced my face as I thought of the surprise awaiting them. This would be a very special hike, and their surprise would surface in due time. In the meanwhile, the chamisa offered a poignant counterpoint to my mood. I would be flying down to Florida on business. Trapped in a metal cylinder at speeds and altitudes we have no right to be experiencing, air travel has always been hard. It is so disconnected from life. That struggle was still three weeks away, which left time to focus on the here and now.

The trip began on a mesa hilltop at 5,600 feet overlooking a narrow two-hundred-foot deep valley carved by a meager stream slowly meandering through rigid black basalt. Terrye had "discovered" this trail through conversations with friends. The parking lot was unofficial, and on either BLM land or tribal land of the Cochiti Pueblo. We really did not know. However, the spot attracted many people due to the sheer vertical sides of the canyon. It was clear that rock climbers had claimed this site for weekend recreation. We joined the crowd in anticipation of a good day.

Dropping down the steep boot-beaten path to the winding creek, we were surrounded by climbers, their colorful garb, and bright ribbons of rope. While they practiced fascinating moves on the sheer rock, we took the path least traveled toward the Monument. It made all the difference. Within minutes the walls of the canyon closed in, and we picked our way back and forth across the creek. The stream was bordered by a profusion of green grass and cattails. Another couple of weeks and things would be turning brown. Slender willows reached for the sky and made the trail difficult to discern in the confusion of plants. And just like that, the silence of wildness closed upon us.

A canyon wren trilled occasionally in celebrating the joy of a warming fall morning. An azure sky, one of New Mexico's signatures, was limitless above us. Bill, in the lead, was doing a brain drain on Terrye. Thus, there were comforting sights before me not only in friends, but the landscape as well. We were walking up a narrow valley bordered on each side by steep basalt walls of porous brown-black rock. A stream flowed down the middle between the thirty-yard-wide crease in the plateau. Our path was simultaneously hidden and then blatantly obvious depending on the density of the riparian vegetation. This should be extremely good rattlesnake habitat.

Our trail and canyon turned to the northeast. West were buttes and mesas at six thousand feet, eventually climbing toward the Jemez Mountains. To the direct north lay Bandelier National Monument, and to the vast east flowed the Rio Grande—at this moment rather sluggish while it waited for replenishment from winter snows.

The Monument is a fabulous collection of high southwestern mesas and canyons winding east toward the Rio Grande. Canyons begin well up in the Jemez Mountains at roughly nine thousand feet and slope dramatically toward the river. In spring these canyons are alive with burbling creeks carrying snowmelt to the Rio Grande. In summer, they funnel the dramatic largess of thunderstorms toward an inevitable mingling with waters coming down from Colorado. This is classic high-mesa country with the wonderful addition of a mountain range backdrop. Forested hills sweep down onto high mesas of ponderosa and piñon. Canyons two hundred to four hundred feet deep, rich with undergrowth and sheltering trees along the streams, cleave the mesas. As the canyons themselves lose elevation, vegetation turns sparse with hardy stands of juniper and piñon as anchors.

A terrific aspect of this country is the combination of just enough forest, vegetation, and water to soften the view. Yet the fundamentally arid character of the country is all too apparent, with brilliant light dominating the landscape. Of course, this is why we were hiking to Bandelier in fall. There are really only two seasons—spring and fall—when walking is a joy. Snow at this elevation makes winter a challenge, and the summer sun is merciless. Summer also presents the hazard of thunderstorms that form above the Jemez crest and then roll off the mountains down toward Santa Fe and the Sangre de Cristos.

In the middle reaches of Bandelier's canyons, ponderosa pines provide shade and a pine-needle carpet. Canyon valleys offer protection from strong winds and trails are softened by the pine needles and the chalky white pumice that lies beneath them. Mountain mahogany, chamisa, desert olive, mullein, bluestem, mountain muhly, and locust grow in profusion in the canyons when shade and water are found in the right combinations. Squirrels, chipmunks, snakes, and birds are abundant. Deer are drawn down from the mountains to sample rich grasses on the mesas. Coyotes' cries are not just a lament for Santa Fe. They must also be proclaiming their happiness with life at the Monument—plenty of food and water.

As if the sheer beauty of the canyons, mesas, mountains, and forests was not enough, Bandelier Monument is blessed with another jewel. Indigenous people occupied this land extensively from A.D. 1075 to 1550. Ruins and pottery shards are found throughout the landscape, and tufa rock walls of ancient settlements are visible along many of the trails. The most prevalent indicator is an ant colony that has taken up residence within the infill of a former room. Some of the ruins are enormous, though only remaining as a heap of blocks amid junipers, oaks, and ponderosa pines. Fallen structures trap moisture that in turn feeds the trees. In a distant past many trod these pumice paths in the course of a typical day—going down to the stream for water, setting out for a hunt, tending a field, or watching for interlopers.

Spring is the best time to search for ruins and pottery shards because frost levitates the pottery to the surface for all to see. Varied hues and patterns characterize these vestiges of a forgotten time. The pottery encourages introspection on how tough life was before the conveniences we take for granted. This is such a special land, but it can be unforgiving on a broiling hot day or ice-cold night. There is no idealized bucolic past here. Life was hard and short. But it too must have possessed its good measure of sweet breezes in spring, the warmth of a summer night, and the beauty of looking across the great Rio Grande to see the Sangre de Cristos after their first snowfall.

Large pueblo structures, the Painted Cave toward which we labored, and various shrines are the most notable traces of a rich heritage. The Shrine of the Stone Lions includes two mountain lions carved in pumice stone. To this day, Native people, New Age spiritualists, and the curious visit the shrines to pay their respects. It is not uncommon to find pottery shards, deer antlers, prayer sticks, and other tokens left in honor at the shrines. Respect is the watchword, but it is impossible to control what happens at the sacred sites located in the middle of the wilderness. Of course, these lands are not wilderness in the traditional sense. People have been living on the Pajarito Plateau and its mesas and canyon for more than a thousand years. Despite this occupation, the land is wild in the most positive sense of the word.

An outline of six-thousand-foot-high buttes marched northward before us as we walked through the canyons and skirted a butte reminiscent of Monument Valley, aglow in muted shades of ivory, brown, and red rock. The canyon bottom was littered with tracks of cattle and their concomitant fouling of the watercourse. A good summer rain would take care of this mess. Still, the wildness of the land was violated and the presence of humans was apparent in subtle ways—a long deteriorated roadway here, a long sheet of corrugated aluminum there, and remains of a barbed-wire fence in places. All of this would fall away at the Monument, and the land would lose these modern intrusions.

We dropped down toward the Rio Grande with the sun at full strength. In the wash coming down from Sanchez Canyon, we stopped for a snack and to adjust our clothing. The Rio Grande flowed up to this canyon in a slim extended arm. Light brown water was pulsing with small waves, various sticks and vegetable matter floating there in the protected bay.

I took time to gather a sprig of chamisa. Its yellow-gold flowers were pungent and in full bloom of musty bouquet. I found a cottonwood twig with a gnarly lump on the stem. A small piece of black obsidian surfaced in the sand. Further scouting turned up a lump of pine pitch. All of these small mementos would go with me to Florida. At the lodge I would spread them out on the nightstand to rekindle memories of home. A break in the business meetings often found me back at my room with time to smell the scents of land thousands of miles to the west. Memorabilia also stimulated pleasant daydreams during the slower parts of the meetings. They affirmed a commitment to return the gifts I had borrowed.

To the northeast we looked up Sanchez Canyon. A half-mile wide where it ended at the Rio Grande, Sanchez Canyon narrowed to one-quarter mile at a point three miles farther up before bending and blending into the mountains. Terrye remarked that it would be fun to explore this canyon. Yes indeed. There is no trail noted on the topographical map. Ruins are noted on the mesa above this defile. What must it have been like in those days past? Was there more water in Sanchez Canyon than today? If not, it would be a long trek to the Rio Grande or down to another water source.

We climbed once again only to drop back down to the Rio Grande in order to begin a long mile across the rock-strewn landscape toward Capulin Canyon. Medio Canyon, into which we had just dropped, was twisted and contorted. But it too held the same promise of fabulous exploration demonstrated by Sanchez Canyon. How fun it would be to set up a base camp down here and to explore for several days. However, there is great speculation about how much radioactive contamination actually has invaded Bandelier National Monument from Los Alamos. Contamination has been detected in some of the streams and canyons closer to the facilities. Tests after the great fire of 2000 show alarming levels of contaminants. The government assures us that there is no danger—that's a comforting thought. This is an amazing juxtaposition of a long-recognized sacred mesa—a place of great spirituality—versus the atomic contamination of contemporary society.

Just when we thought that the heat was becoming unpleasant, clouds began to form over the Jemez. Gone was the warmth, and fall reasserted itself. A fence line and signs conveyed the boundary of the Monument and warned visitors to respect the laws governing the resources. Despite these warnings I took back many things—the sound of the increasing wind in the pines in Capulin Canyon, the smell of decaying leaves by the stream, the silence of wildness, the warmth of heat radiating off rocks and pumice, and the knowledge that others had been here long before me and had stolen these same treasures before the federal government had even existed.

We had a little over a mile and a quarter to go before reaching the cave. Cloud cover dropped the temperature several notches. The trail entered the best of Capulin Canyon. At the mouth of the canyon are scattered ponderosa pines, piñon, and junipers, which encourage dense growth of chamisa, Apache plume, and oak. Meanwhile, the trail remains close to a gurgling creek with its characteristic milky color. Birds became more vocal and prevalent within the safety of the canyon. All eyes scanned the hillside trying to locate the cave in the dense vegetation.

The trail turned a bit through the piñon and junipers, and there was Painted Cave about fifty feet up on the north side of Capulin Canyon— not exactly a cave, but a shallow depression in a volcanic wall. The depression is deep enough that its overhang protects the back surface from weather and sun. Many drawings depicting stars, hands, crosses, and buildings can be seen below the arched roof. Red, black, and white dominate the stylized drawings. Although some may be true petroglyphs and the work of the Anasazi, the authenticity of the paintings is doubtful. What really counts is the sense of history belonging to the canyon. Whether drawn by Anasazi, Pueblo Indian, Spanish explorers, or shepherds, the pictographs convey a sense of timelessness to Painted Cave and Capulin Canyon. They serve as a vivid reminder that people have continually been drawn to this canyon across time.

It is impossible to stand there in the shelter of Capulin Canyon looking up at the paintings without realizing how special this site, and Bandelier Monument as a whole, is. The unique spirit of the mesas, canyons, water, trees, shrubs, and wildlife is distinctive and easily distinguishable from other wild places. Here is an uncanny intersection among natural beauty, human celebration, and spiritual power.

The base of the cave is littered with rockfall from the cliff and the remains of rock dwellings from the past. As might be expected, trees in this area are rather small—twenty feet high or so—because former occupants of the area cleared the site for habitation. Rain did not seem to be a threat despite the cloudy sky, so we found several logs and sat down to enjoy our meal.

At the start of the day, Terrye and Bill had asked why I was carrying my backpack instead of the daypack. I simply said that I wanted to carry extra water, clothing, and food and I felt that the backpack would be more comfortable. It was time to spring my surprise. Before they could pull out their lunches, I asked for assistance. "Bill, will you get this stove going for me?" "Are you going to have soup?" he asked. "No not quite. Just light the stove please." "Terrye, could you please get this bottle opened?" And then they began to understand the plan.

I had brought along a bottle of Sangria. The first course of our lunch would be chips and salsa. Out came a bag of blue corn tortilla chips that Bill gladly opened. The salsa was my type of salsa—mild. Terrye and Bill shouted with joy for this surprise. I poured the Sangria and wondered about the Monument regulations concerning alcohol. We would each have a small glass—just enough to accompany our meal, but not enough to cause any problems or to desecrate the spirit of this place.

"Go easy on that first course please." "We will be having hot chili and warmed tortillas if we ever get this stove working." Bill concentrated on the stove and soon it was blasting. "Howard, this is a great surprise," exclaimed Bill. "What a wonderful treat," added Terrye. I cut up tomatoes and lettuce to garnish the chili. Cheese was grated on top of the chili to add yet another counterpoint. "Fix this as you please." "Here are knives and forks. The paper plates and napkins are inside the pack if you will pull them out, Terrye."

And thus, my friends were treated to a meal that they never dreamed would materialize that day. Sitting back in this ancient site, enjoying a fine meal was definitely an unanticipated treat. We were just tired enough that a rest was warranted. Here among the ruins and among friends, we toasted Capulin Canyon. As we finished the second course I rummaged through the pack to pull out the third and final course—chocolate pudding.

After such a fine and filling meal we struggled to get going again. My pack was lighter for the aid of my friends. Nonetheless, lethargy permeated our group. We struggled up the hill out of the canyon and began the descent toward Medio Canyon. Sometime after Sanchez Canyon the filling effects of food and grog wore off. We methodically put one foot in front of another to reach the car. However, we would not soon forget this meal, our companionship, or the spirit of place in a special corner of New Mexico.

Our next trip to this Bandelier gateway would be our last, although we had no way of knowing it at the time. From many perspectives it was perhaps the best trip. Three of us squeezed into my old four-wheel-drive Chevy pickup with only 117,000 miles; it was just becoming broken in. This early November day was brisk, with a few clouds scudding along in the sky. Breezes rose and fell all day. It was perfect for hiking.

Just past the small community of Cochiti, we turned off on the dirt road that would lead to the trailhead. A steep grade rises about fifty feet and then the road levels out. We negotiated muddy pools on the way in since the area had seen quite a bit of rain in recent days. At the trailhead the usual collection of hiker and climber cars were found. How some were able to drive passenger cars through the mud and the muck is beyond me. But, there they were. We had decided to wander back toward Bandelier Monument but there was no specific destination in mind.

We dropped down the steep hillside into the canyon and streambed. Within minutes we had left behind the commotion of the rock climbers. It felt good to stretch and empty our minds after a week at work. Wildness has a distinct restorative power. I opened my spirit to the beauty around me.

A barbed-wire fence blocked the middle of the canyon. Perhaps fifty yards away from this boundary line a fellow in his late sixties materialized from behind a drought-stricken juniper. A cowboy hat, western shirt, jeans, and boots were well worn—this was no urban cowboy. He leased land from the University of New Mexico for a well-known apple orchard. Walking the fence line, he also ran cattle on the leased land. This was a tough old hombre who did not like the looks of us at all.

"Do you know you are trespassing?"

"No, not really," said Bill. "We were just walking up to Bandelier National Monument. We thought this was BLM land."

"Well, it isn't. You're on the Dixon Ranch."

"We're sorry," replied Bill, "We mean no harm and we are just passing through."

"Where did you start from?"

"We began over by the golf course," said Terrye coming to Bill's rescue. Good timing. The situation looked like it needed a little feminine charm.

"You ain't by chance University professors?" Before we could reply he said, "I keep my eye out for those professors. I have one who is intent on coming on my land to rob pots and graves."

Bless her heart. Terrye spoke right up, "Heavens no, I work for the gas company." He paused and scrutinized us, mulling over her reply.

"Have you ever been to the Stone Lions?" he asked. Bill said, "Yes, we have all been there before, we just are out for some exercise." That response apparently did the trick.

"Well, let me tell you about another stone lion that few even know about. You see that butte over there? No, that one behind the small isolated mesa. Yeah, that one. Climb up to the top and you will find a shrine that is seldom visited compared to the Shrine of the Stone Lions. Just don't disturb anything and next time ask for permission to cross my land."

"Thanks so much for your permission and the tip. We are indebted to you. We'll be over later for apples."

We turned collectively and headed up the wash. What luck. Perhaps we would find a new discovery and in the process have a bit of adventure. Yes, the day was looking up after all.

The trail wound in and out of several canyons with the mesas towering above us. Heading off the trail opened new delights, but it also made the going tougher. Apache plume and chamisa created an irregular path up a wash toward the target mesa. We would have to climb five hundred feet to the mesa top. It didn't look like much of a challenge, but the steepness of the jutting mesa was proving a challenge. Fallen blocks of tuff that we negotiated in the steep upward ascent replaced the sandy wash.

Without any precise location of the stone lion in mind, this hike became a new adventure. We knew what we were looking for and where it might be found in the general vicinity. Certainly lurking in the back of our minds was the possibility that we had been sent on a wild goose chase. No matter. The hunt was fun, and we walked on in eager anticipation.

Terrye was in the lead on the final stretch up a defile in the mesa. As we reached the last twenty feet before the rim of the mesa, we were blocked by near vertical rock. Bill found a possible way up that turned out to be of no use. I finally discovered a spot where two quick moves up the rock face would put us on top. Exposure was excessive but with a few quick moves I scrambled for the safety of the rim. "Just do it," I yelled down. "Don't stop to think about it or you'll never make it. Try to take it all in one movement." Terrye nimbly rose to the lip of the rim and I offered a hand up. Bill decided to make more deliberate moves on yet another passage and soon reached the safety of our waiting arms.

We gazed out on the Rio Grande Valley, where the weather was still cloudless with a slight wind. The warming sun felt good as we basked in the radiance of a perfect fall day. The sapphire blue New Mexico sky seemed endless. To the northeast spread the Sangre de Cristos, with Lake Peak and Santa Fe Baldy dominating the skyline. The Truchas Peaks were mantled in snow to the north of our old friends. It would be another year before those trails would reappear. To the southeast stood the ramparts of the Sandia Mountains, while the higher Jemez Mountains loomed in the west. I could see for a hundred miles to the south. The perspiration of the climb chilled in the soft breeze and we snapped back to the present.

We spread out in hopes of finding the stone lion. This was turning out to be more difficult than we initially figured. On top of the huge mesa with scattered juniper and piñon trees, it was just not clear where the lion might be found. The rock almost blended into one shade of dirty vanilla. What might be natural and human-made blurred. After ten minutes of rooting around and nearing the northeast edge of the mesa, I was about ready to give up. That's when eagle-eyed Terrye shouted out, "Here it is."

Bill and I scrambled over to the stone lion. It was considerably more eroded than the shrine in Bandelier National Monument. But beyond this deterioration, it was clear that the lion was still revered by people. Pottery shards and prayer sticks were numerous and reverently placed for the spirits. My mind drifted to those who carved out this site overlooking the Rio Grande. At the edge of the mesa, it was easy to see how it was protected in earlier times and probably designated as off-limits in everyday life. The difficulty in climbing up on the mesa also contributed to its rigor and safety. I tried to envision the ceremonies, perhaps early in the morning as the sun crested the distant mountains, and those many eyes drawn to the scenic splendor around them. Like us they knew little of the after life, but they certainly recognized and worshiped the spirit of this place. Were we really all that much different?

Pulling out our lunches, we backed off to the shade of a huge spreading juniper. A chilling breeze spiraled down from the Jemez Mountains. What would the ancient ones have thought about the convenience we enjoy today? Here we were with our easily prepared foods. Our high-tech gear would have been coveted by the elders—or would it? Insulating ourselves from the natural world has brought with it as many, if not more, problems, and the loss of a sense of spirituality. Is the loss really worth the cost?

The way back was uneventful. We wound down the mesa's crumbling sides, dodging chamisa, cholla, and Apache plume. On our way back the canyon washes flew by. Beneath the vertical cliffs of basalt, the climbers hung over us and shouted to one another in boisterous glee. "Climbing." "Off belay." Climbers played out their heroics there on the cliffs. We reached the base of the canyon and climbed the hundred feet to the top. Time for refreshments.

In the truck, we drove through an enormous puddle back toward the paved road. The day was beginning to wane, and we all felt a deep sense of satisfaction having shared camaraderie among the ancient ones and ourselves. Around one curve, down a dip, and we started to climb the slight incline before the last fifty feet drop to the road. "Hey, what's this?" cried Bill. There at the apex of the road was a steel cable drawn between two posts blocking the road. The rusted posts had been there for a very long time. The cable was new. We then realized that the land was not BLM land but part of Cochiti Pueblo. "What should we do now?" I asked. "Just go over to our left around that hump and we will find a way down to the pavement," said Bill. I wasn't so sure we would find a way down. Terrye got out of the truck and walked along the ridge. She directed me to a steep cut in the bank. I shifted into four-wheel drive and dropped down the precipitous slope. We would have to find new entrances to Bandelier in the future.

New Mexico possesses a spirituality of place that is palpable to those who live there and those who pause to visit. Certainly many are only superficially cognizant of this spiritual power. They do not see past the fun and funkiness of Santa Fe nor the incredible serenity of a high mountain stream filled with native trout as it serenades its way through a meadow. They only gaze with wonder at the ruins of Native settlements without understanding the sense of place that permeates the pueblo adobe walls, kiva ceremonials, and historic trading routes. They fail to see the connection between the location of an Anasazi settlement and an early trade route in the history of humankind.

Bandelier National Monument is more than just a pretty assemblage of high-desert mesas, rough arroyos, and ancient inhabitations. It represents a special place in the geography of New Mexico where the spiritual power of the earth reveals itself in an incredible pallet of colors, shapes, surfaces, smells, temperatures, and light. One thousand years ago indigenous people recognized this power and embraced the land. Their culture was connected intimately with the earth. As a result, they built various shrines such as the Stone Lions and the Painted Cave. Couldn't we benefit from their insight and love for this beautiful land, as well as their willingness to celebrate the spirituality of place?

5
Close Encounters of the Furry Kind

Darkness had finally arrived, and with it the prospects of rest after an arduous day of driving. It was hard to believe that I had actually arrived in Grand Teton National Park, one of the penultimate mountain reserves. Huddled in the little log cabin on sparkling Colter Bay, penetrating cold began to seep through the walls. It might be summer in New Mexico, but here in Wyoming late May was still early spring. Snowdrifts under the trees around the cabin confirmed that warm weather was just a theory in Jackson Hole. Pure cold air almost hurt as I breathed in the essence of the Tetons. Alive with a special feeling about this querencia, I felt the spirits of the Tetons call.

Who has visited the Grand Tetons, Yellowstone, Glacier National Park, Mount Rainier, Grand Canyon, or another place of great natural beauty and not been touched by the spirit of place? In the case of Jackson Hole and the Grand Tetons, it is just too easy to be mesmerized by a tangible spirit of mountain life. The Teton Range looms over Jackson Lake with its spires reaching lofty heights in the brilliant sunshine. All sorts of wildlife including bison, moose, elk, swans, and various waterfowl are easily visible to the most hurried travelers. In fact, it would be very difficult for even the most callous person to visit this spot on earth without recognizing that there is something exceedingly unique, something extraordinary in spirit about the Tetons.

In *Teewinot,* Jack Turner chronicles his love for the Tetons and their captivating spirit. Turner describes his yearnings for the vagaries of the seasons that often spell snow in summer; the spires to which he guides clients; the hut in the saddle between the Grand and Middle Teton; the simple plywood cabin that he resurrects from winter in early May from the lasting snow drifts; the mountain lion that tracks him while skiing; and, the wonderful promenade of visitors along park roads in early April before motor vehicles are permitted. What makes Turner's story so compelling is the sum of its parts—Jackson Hole and Teton National Park reflect a distinctive personality and spirit.

Terry Tempest Williams has similarly shared a passionate tale about the Bear River Migratory Bird Refuge in Utah and its recovery from flood. *Refuge* captures the spirit of wildlife and family in response to natural disasters. The life of the refuge becomes a metaphor for the life of her family. Within the refuge Williams discovers the spirit of renewal, a spirit that nurtures and sustains her own attempts at grieving and restoration. It is the spirituality of place to which Williams is drawn and from which she draws sustenance for life.

The ideas conveyed by Turner and Williams are very similar, even though their books are substantially different. Both give us an appreciation of a special place that is their heart's joy—a querencia. Although the physical qualities of place are radically different—high-desert Salt Lake versus Rocky Mountain range—each acknowledges the extraordinary spirit of place that comforts their souls. A culture that embraces the earth can seek the spirituality of place and benefit from its tangible presence. We simply need to improve our receptivity in recognizing the obvious.

At twenty-four yards, the dark brown coat of Bear Number 367—all numbers have been changed to protect the innocent—glistened with the gathering moisture of another drizzly afternoon in Glacier National Park and the waning summer. I took a step closer to the backcountry ranger at my side and glanced at his pack harness, armed with a magnum can of pepper spray. I knew I could not outrun the grizzly bear because she was in her prime, but could I outrun him? After all, he would be the one to deploy the pepper spray, thus raising the ire of this magnificent creature.

The ranger used his portable radio to call in a warning to headquarters. This was one trail that would be closed immediately. Bear Number 367 had committed the unforgivable transgression of threatening the lives of park visitors. Yet no one could have walked away from that scene without knowing that the very breath of life had touched him or her deeply, indelibly, and spiritually.

The ranger finished his call and began a recitation of the facts surrounding Bear Number 367. She was a three-year-old female who might have cubs in another two years. She tended to follow her mother's habit of browsing among berry bushes along Iceberg Lake Trail in late summer, a mere ten minutes away by foot from Swiftcurrent Motor Inn and the trailhead parking lot. This proclivity to dine in the immediate proximity of the visiting hordes was a learned, habituated behavior.

These facts seemed irrelevant as the rain rolled from her fur. At the lower range of three hundred pounds, Bear Number 367 had clearly succeeded in finding the sort of nutrition she needed to survive another brutal winter. Her mother had taught her well, and from all indications she would soon be passing her encyclopedia of bear knowledge on to her offspring. Would they be as majestic as she?

Asked how he knew this biography about Bear Number 367, the ranger replied that he was the backcountry bear ranger. What luck! If you are going to meet a grizzly bear at close quarters, then you definitely want to have your own personal specialist ranger along. Out of curiosity, I questioned him about what other gear he might be carrying in his pack besides the radio. The ranger hesitated a moment and said, "I also carry a .44 caliber magnum. But by the time I could get it out of the pack she would have killed both of us." Suddenly those twenty-four yards shrank to nothing. Here was the top of the food chain casually munching on berries. At any moment she could have her way with me. She slightly moved her gaze in our direction. The ranger continued, "She knows perfectly well that we are here. She has sized us up and is not threatened so long as we do not invade her sense of safe distance. Take one step off the trail toward her and that would probably be enough." I edged another half step alongside and behind the ranger.

The hike had started innocently enough. With the driving behind me, I was ready to enjoy a moment of solitude and exercise. Three days earlier we had landed in Kalispell, Montana. After negotiating the blighted maze of strip malls, fast food stores, and other detritus of commercial Kalispell, we arrived at Lake McDonald Lodge and our base for two days.

Midmorning of the third day we headed up the Going-To-The-Sun Highway, except that the sun was nonexistent. Heavy overcast skies dominated the park. As we approached Logan Pass the temperature plummeted, resulting in one of the world's shortest stops at the visitor center because it was too cold—just above freezing—to enjoy the view. Those who were among the less prepared on touring bikes dominated the center itself. They had bought into summer and were thrust into dangerous early winter conditions. Their plight became more tenuous when they started down the road as the wind chill created intolerable conditions. Most were walking and thumbing rides down to Lake St. Mary.

By early afternoon I was tired, hungry, and cultivating a massive headache from eye strain and negotiating traffic. The fabled Many

Close Encounters of the Furry Kind

Glacier Hotel materialized at just the right moment. After settling in, we met in the lobby and sorted out the afternoon—browsing in the hotel shop, sleeping, and reading were the preferences. I exited to the trailhead behind Swiftcurrent Motor Inn. I carried a modest daypack, including the bare minimum for these conditions, and a shelled coat; the pack contained a wool cap and gloves that provide a measured range of safety in these conditions. It was not quite raining, and having just come down from Logan Pass I knew that limited precipitation was likely to fall—only the temperature and some mist were likely to drop.

Of course, we laughed at all the hikers around the Lodge who were wearing these tinkling bells—bear bells to alert bears of the hikers' presence. They seemed like a rather extreme measure to take on such a popular hike like Iceberg Lake Trail. I had encountered lots of bears in my years hiking and roaming mountains. It was unlikely that I would so much as see a bear in the vast distance in the middle of the afternoon. I told the folks to relax and that I would see them later.

All of the witty criticisms about the bear bells, bravado assurances, and macho thoughts began to evaporate as I pulled up to the trailhead. Posted at the beginning of the trail was the Park Service's warning that a bear had been frequenting the trail. We laughed at these signs when we first saw them at Yellowstone Park. The caricature is comical—a ferocious beast with oversized claws prominently displayed and oversized fangs ready to rip the nearest human to pieces. "Ha, ha, ha," we laughed. The Park Service is trying to protect us from ourselves. It is extremely rare to see a grizzly bear even from a distance.

I played this knowledge over in my head as I started up the trail. "No big deal. Been to the big-time mountains and done that. Seen black bears at very close range. Seen big black bears at very close range. Seen mothers with cubs at close range. Ho hum." That false bravado began to erode the minute I encountered the first three hikers heading out. They were all wearing bear bells. They were carrying on a very loud conversation. Suddenly I felt very exposed. Not in a group—not good. Not wearing noisemakers like bear bells—not good. Steep slope to my right with all sorts of bluffs that hindered sight uphill—not good. Dense brush down to the left that was tall enough to obscure the sight of large mobile objects—not good. Slight mist/drizzle masking sounds—not good. Wet trail that dampened sounds—not good.

The sights, sounds, and smells of trails vary extensively, and I was progressing with my attention to these differences while recuperating from too much social contact in recent days. Whether to focus on the beauty of this valley with the looming peaks ahead or simply to detoxify myself from social overindulgence was a difficult choice. I could sense the potential beauty of Glacier National Park, but in reality I had yet to see the stupendous mountains and ridges for which the park is internationally known. As I came up out of one slight crease in the mountain, I saw three people ahead on the trail.

The closer I came to these three individuals, the more I sensed that something was terribly wrong. Two of them, a young man and a woman, were gesticulating wildly with their arms and pointing in several directions. "Hey, wait a minute. That's a ranger they are talking to. I wonder what the excitement is all about?" At ten yards I could see the terror in their faces. With eyes as big as saucers, they pointed down into the valley and the wonderful creek. I ambled up and said hello. The fellow in the ranger outfit with a pack and radio antenna sticking out concisely defined the situation: "This couple has just seen a grizzly bear." We scanned the willow-choked creek bottom, but there was no evidence of any bear. At that point, my senses were as attuned to the outdoors as they possibly could be given the situation. My hearing, sight, and smell were all attenuated. Where is that bear? How could it just disappear?

Our ranger laid out the choices. "They are headed out. I am continuing on up to Ptarmigan Falls. Which way are you going?" "Hey, duh! That's a no-brainer." I thought to myself, "You have the bear spray on your pack strap. I'm going to go back with this freaked-out couple? No way." "I am heading up to the Falls as well. Mind if I join you?" And, thus I found myself hiking with Glacier National Park's backcountry bear ranger. Out of professional courtesy, I let him take the lead.

I cannot remember much of our conversation. Maybe we did not converse much. I was only aware of his clapping hands and shouts of "Hey bear" as we rounded corners of the trail or entered stands of timber. His pace was mild and I felt no strain to keep up. Clearly he was seeking the safety of my companionship. Safety in numbers. Surely my presence did wonders for his confidence.

As we passed hiking groups coming out of the backcountry, all with bear bells, he merely said "good afternoon." He provided no warning of a potential bear ahead. Perhaps he did not trust the sighting of the couple, or maybe he concluded that it could have been a black bear just as well as a grizzly. I did not let the ranger out of my sight.

Close Encounters of the Furry Kind

At the Falls the weather began to turn worse. Mist changed to rain, and I switched from a flannel shirt to a nylon-shelled coat with a polyester liner. The ranger commented, "Oh, you are more prepared than I thought." I guess I must have looked like a tourist or something since I was wearing jeans (cotton) and a flannel shirt (cotton) in conditions that warranted something along the lines of wool or polyester. The rain was significant enough for me to add the wool cap. It looked like another familiar trudge out in rainy conditions—something I was too familiar with having spent years in the Pacific Northwest. Hunker down and grind out the miles. The ranger set a faster pace going out. It was then when we were about ten minutes from the trailhead that we rounded a corner in the trail and there she was. "Wow."

All I could focus on was this dark brown head with long snout methodically harvesting berries at a frantic pace. For the most part she kept broadside to the trail allowing us to see her full features. Occasionally after ripping off berries with an upward thrust, she would stand there munching them and cast a glance sideways in our direction. But eye contact was never established. What an incredible feeling. I was both awed and terrified to see a grizzly this close. Neither the ranger nor I said anything for the longest time, as we stood transfixed by the sight before us. Perhaps she sensed our respect.

Apparently the berries she was consuming were more than plentiful, since she hardly moved. It would be incorrect to say that the grizzly was browsing, because she essentially had commandeered this patch of earthly delights. It was extremely quiet, with only the mist hitting my jacket to break up the silence other than the pounding thuds of heartbeats from ranger and hiker. In time the mist began to stop with a slight breaking up in the overcast. I turned to the ranger and he just smiled.

Within ten more minutes a middle-aged couple came down the trail and about ran us over. "What's up?" The ranger replied very casually, "Oh, we're just watching the grizzly down there." How had they missed it? Now that it was on their radar screen, they grew extremely excited. As her partner dug his binoculars out of his pack, the woman explained to me that they had been visiting Glacier National Park for twenty years and had never seen a grizzly. They lived in Livingston, Montana, where she was a schoolteacher. This would be one fine story for her students to hear about. They took turns sharing the binoculars and then she asked me if I wanted to borrow them. There was nothing to miss— not the fangs, not the claws, not the muscled hump.

Another party soon arrived, and the ranger began to grow anxious. "We are getting too many people here. With this close proximity we want to minimize our threat to her. It's time for you to be moving along." Everyone just stood there staring at the gorgeous bear. Here was a once-in-a-lifetime encounter for some; a once-in-a-twenty-year encounter for others; and just another grizzly for the ranger. Well, that's not quite how he responded, despite having had hundreds, if not thousands, of bear encounters in the course of his job. There was absolutely no impression that this was just another bear. The ranger demonstrated no less respect and fascination than did the rest of us. He, too, was clearly in love with the bear.

As another group came around the corner, I volunteered to leave. There were simply too many people on top of this bear. As I turned and reluctantly left, the bear glanced one last time in my direction. Well, okay. She was looking at all of us, but I felt that indescribable communication that occurs between human and animal. I had been touched deeply forever by the experience, and she had the grace to honor the encounter by a farewell glance in my direction. I proceeded down the trail, not really touching the ground. Here was the experience that every outdoors person relishes—contact with a big, dominant mammal that could kill you in an instant if it wanted to do so.

As if to honor this great moment, the sun began to shine. What had been a dark and gloomy day now was all brightness and cheer. As I reached the trailhead, three teenage girls were starting up the initial switchbacks. "Be careful," I said, "I just ran into a grizzly about ten minutes up the trail." That stopped them in their tracks.

That evening after a delicious meal we left the cozy dining room of Many Glacier Hotel for the porch to gaze out on Swiftcurrent Lake. The temperature was cool—in the low fifties—with a variable breeze, but not too windy or cold. We stood looking with wonder on the fantastic tableau—the recently snow-covered peaks reaching to the sky, the deep blue-green lake, and the green valley and mountain shoulders that soon would lose their sheen with the changing season. I glassed the hillside to the immediate east. There was dense brush growing one-third of the way up the mountainside before the rock and scree became dominant. I looked into one patch of dense brush growing to about five feet tall. There was a big brown furry back working its way slowly through the green vegetation. "Look, everyone," I said. "There's a brown bear over there to the east about thirty yards up from the road."

My father replied, "That's not brown, it's black." "You're crazy," I said. "Yes, it's over there by the trees." "No, it's up in the bushes." Only then did we realize that there were two bears. Well, there were more like four bears on that hillside. That must have been some very fine berry eating to attract all of these bruins. People were walking casually along the road for their postdinner constitutional. They had no idea that bears were literally a few feet from them munching berries and having a grand old time.

The bear spectacle continued. Although not alarmed by the passing people, they were highly alert to each other. My binoculars were not powerful enough to ascertain whether the bears were grizzly or black bears, or both. What an incredible park this was. I have never seen so many bears in one spot. It was a perfect ending to a fun-filled day.

The night passed uneventfully, and the next day dawned with clouds and gray skies. The swirling dark masses over the peaks gave a clear sign that fall was on its way, if not here. I slipped out of the room while everyone else slept and went down to the lake to see what I might see. Alas, panning across all of the mountainsides, I could see no large mammals. No matter where I looked, there was just the gray-green of early dawn. No one else was up and about, and for good reason. The freezing wind was not fun by any stretch of the imagination. Still, here I was in one of the most beautiful parks in the world. That was pretty good solace. I had to savor the moment because it might be some time before I would be here again.

I turned my attention to the lake and loons swimming across toward the northern shore. The wind whipped up small whitecaps that they rode like a bucking bronco—gracefully up and down amid the tempest. They did not emit their eerie call, but it was nice to know that I had seen the embodiment of that unforgettable sound. Without the slightest warning, a small squall blew in, dropping freezing mist, and ended my birdwatching. Glacier Park in late summer can be a mighty good friend, and a challenging foe at a moment's notice.

Morning slowly went by with wet and windy conditions. After lunch I took a ranger-guided hike to Grinnell Lake. We boarded a small boat at the dock that carried us across Swiftcurrent Lake. By the time the ten-minute ride was through, the sun was beginning to come out and the skies were clearing into a brilliant blue. A stiff wind was slowly dissipating. When we docked, it was as if another day had dawned. The ranger led us to Lake Josephine and our next boat.

Five

Sitting in the rear of the thirty-foot boat as it chugged slowly across the mile-long lake, we had plenty of opportunity to scan the hillsides with our binoculars. At our launching point a trail headed upward toward the pass and glaciers. Although we did not take it, I glassed the route for future consideration.

As I located the trail I saw a pair of hikers ambling along. Then I scanned the hillside above them. An enormous brown bear was grazing about four hundred yards above them. They had no clue what they were missing as the steep hillside blocked their view. I could not believe the prevalence of bears in this park. I just wished I had more powerful binoculars to distinguish between the grizzlies and black bears. I spotted a couple of white specks to the west of the hikers and down on a rock outcropping. It turned out to be a small band of mountain goats now luxuriating in the warm sun. The emerald green grasses amid the rocks shone with health and vitality—gifts from the precipitation.

The boat landed at a dock and our party of fifteen people followed the ranger's instructions to assemble. He would lead us on a short twenty-minute hike to Grinnell Lake with a view up to the glaciers. He repeated the warning that we were in grizzly bear habitat and to exercise appropriate caution. With that said, he started down the trail. His cries of "Hey bear" floated to us in the rear. A number of obligatory stops were made during which the ranger filled us in on the flora and fauna of Glacier National Park.

We ended at Grinnell Lake, fed by melting snow from a glacier towering above the basin. A modest whisper of a watercourse snaked down several hundred feet from the end of the glacier and splashed harmlessly into the lake. It was a pretty sight, a nice lake in the middle of nowhere. Just the type of lake that would make an excellent campsite if not for the long sleepless night we would have in grizzly territory.

On the way back to Lake Josephine the ranger continued to shout and clap his hands. The trail seldom went straight, and with the dense overhanging brush it was very difficult to see down it. Unfortunately, we never ran into a grizzly grazing in the many damp meadows along the trail. However, as we reached the lakeshore, a young moose was startled from among the reeds and rushes. In its classical gangly fashion the moose headed for the stands of willow and obscurity from the many prying eyes. What a great afternoon it had been following a wet and miserable morning.

Our good fortune for seeing wildlife ended the next day as we returned to Kalispell and the ride home. However, this was not the end of my bear adventures in Glacier National Park. A year later, in late July, I finagled another trip to the park.

One afternoon I decided to hike up Iceberg Lake Trail by Many Glacier Hotel. It was warm that afternoon, in the seventies with a brisk but diminishing wind. The trail was mobbed with others out enjoying a walk in the woods. I reached the site of my previous miraculous encounter and paused. No need to worry about grizzlies at this stage given the heavy foot traffic. Continuing on, I rounded a corner and saw a group of about twenty people, all staring upslope and pointing. Just then a couple of young men came past and said, "Grizzly ahead!"

She was a gigantic bear and looked to be in the range of three hundred and fifty pounds. I say "she" because the crowd of perhaps twenty people included one person who claimed that only females wore the distinctive white crescent collar around the neck. To tell the truth, I had some difficulty in locating her up on the side of the mountain directly above the trail. She was an estimated three hundred yards up the mountainside. Thus, I have my suspicions regarding whether she was actually a female. But who cares? The bear was huge and dominating. Let's assume the bear was a female. She had an interesting mixture of brown coat and head with darker, almost black legs. She was bedded down in a swale of greens. She would lie down and then sit up on her haunches with her front legs straight and stiff.

My most indelible memory is the effect of a fifteen-mile-per-hour wind blowing through her fur. It rippled as she stood up. There she was, just rolling in her bed of rich greens with a cool wind caressing her fur. It was a classic picture, an image that you conjure up when thinking about seeing a grizzly in the backcountry. Huge front legs and paws were coursing through the grass as she rolled around. She obviously was not going anywhere, and yet she seemed so fundamentally purposeful in her repose. As I watched her I could only think about how much bigger she was than the previous grizzly I had seen on this trail. I would not want to get close to this monster—three hundred yards was not too far. Yet the distance added a false sense of security that enabled all there to enjoy her—to savor without that intrusive self-preservation alarm within screaming, "You're dead meat."

I contemplated about how quickly she would be on this group if she wanted to. It would be a steep downhill run that she could complete in mere seconds, that much was certain. Nonetheless, there was a pervading sense of calm among all present—probably a false sense of security. Light and wind played on her as she occasionally munched greens. I was totally taken aback that she would be up on this west-facing slope in the late afternoon for a relatively hot day in Glacier National Park.

I learned that you just couldn't predict where or when you will see these bears. Who saw her in the first place, directly above the trail where you would not be looking? I overheard a short conversation between two fellows who were admiring this feat of the fellow who spotted her. They were taken aback that he spotted her up there on the immensity of the west-facing ridge above Ptarmigan Falls. The lessons were clear: expect everything; open yourself to the possibilities; think like a mountain; think like a bear. Admittedly the rush of adrenaline was not there like the first encounter because the contact was not intimate. That silent, but tangible human-animal communication had not occurred. Still, I knew that she was there, alive and possibly waiting the next time I strolled up the trail in search of furry things.

Glacier National Park is a treasure, its spirit easily discernible to even the first-time visitor. Among its gems are the lofty heights of the Going-To-The-Sun Highway, with tortuous turns and prancing waters of side streams and weeping rocks; the remote location of the park, which makes access difficult and wildness ever-present; the profusion of charismatic wildlife, exemplified by grizzly bears and mountain sheep; the vast trail system, encouraging visitors to leave their vehicles behind; and its classic mountain lodges and chalets, steeped in character and a visible patina of age.

For me there is tremendous value and comfort in knowing that Glacier National Park exists. While future visits may not result in sighting a grizzly bear, I know that the bears are out there. A stay at Many Glacier Hotel may not be as fulfilling because of noisy tenants in one room or another, but other guests cannot rob me of the wind through the conifers, the play of sunlight on the peaks as storm clouds rifle past, or the sound of loons across the lake. Weather may bring gray skies and cold drizzle that dampens enthusiasm for exploring the trails. However, the trails wait there patiently with a bounty of adventure and excitement for the moment that the petty inconveniences are brushed aside.

Just as this tangible spirit of place at Glacier National Park calls to me, so too does the spirit of Jackson Hole and the Grand Tetons. I perk up at the thought of having lunch at Bubba's Barbeque in Jackson Hole before heading to the Taggart Lake trailhead for a little exercise and immersion in the warm, dry foothills at the base of the Tetons. The Snake River will continue to flow casually through the river bottoms with deep browse of willows hiding moose and other wildlife. I can strain with my binoculars in the misty morning glassing the slopes of the mountains across Jackson Lake, looking for a grizzly sow and her cubs on the avalanche slopes far from the intrusion of people. The chill of the night will slowly drive away the waning day and the crisp balsam scented air will remind me that I am on the edge of the wilderness. All of these possibilities add up to a unique place whose spirit brings me immense joy.

Spirituality of place does not manifest itself only in national parks. People merely have an easier time recognizing the tangible distinctive characteristics of places that are achingly beautiful and thoroughly nonurban. A culture that loves the earth will act to set aside and protect special places of uncontested quality that enable us to love the earth. But that is not enough. At the local level, in our communities, towns, and cities, we must also act to protect even tiny places where people can pause to reflect on the strength and serenity of nature. Healed at least for the moment by these querencias of peace and beauty, our spirits can be reborn, allowing us to nurture others as an enlightened society.

A Sense
of
Community

6
The Magic of the Weminuche

In the late 1950s, Colin Fletcher decided to walk the length of California from Algodones, Mexico, to the Warner Mountains of Oregon. The thousand-mile trip lasted half a year. Most people target the Pacific Crest Trail and mountain terrain for such an endeavor, but for more than one-third of the trip Fletcher carried his pack through the California desert. His tale was chronicled in *The Thousand-Mile Summer*, the first of a series describing individual rambles in wild areas.

Fletcher considers himself a compulsive walker, and he quickly followed the thousand-mile jaunt with a now-famous trip through the Grand Canyon. In *The Man Who Walked Through Time*, Fletcher shares his adventurous struggle against loneliness, heat, cold, and thirst. Navigating faint paths and seldom-used trails, Fletcher demonstrated great courage in tackling almost impassable terrain without assistance. He lived to tell about it. *The Man Who Walked Through Time* subsequently became one of the seminal books on nature and required reading for anyone interested in wildness.

Fletcher's last major epic journey was captured in *River*, a tale about his travels along and in the Colorado River from its source to the sea. Like his preceding books, River is beautifully written and enables us to immerse ourselves in his experiences of danger, serenity, wonder, loneliness, melancholy, happiness, and admiration for nature. As with the previous trips, his adventure down the Colorado was solo. In the course of his travels, only occasionally did he spend substantial time in the company of others, when the dangers of travel through massive rapids, extreme desert heat, or high mountain sentinels suggested that companionship was the better part of valor.

Individuals with a record for completing solitary trips have contributed significantly to our understanding of the relationship between humans and nature. Robin Cody canoed down the Columbia River alone, as told in *Voyage of a Summer Sun*, and encountered a wonderful mix of wildness, river culture, and lonely introspection for his efforts. Doug Peacock found personal rehabilitation in the grizzly bears of Yellowstone National Park and other Rocky Mountain habitats. He camped solo in stealth fashion over many years in order to get to know the bears and their ways. His book *Grizzly Years* is a classic account of encounters with the greatest carnivore. Both of these books provide important insights on our relationship with earth, wildness, and life.

The backpacking literature is replete with stories about solo trips over vast distances in wilderness areas. David Cooper hiked alone 120 miles across the Brooks Range in Alaska before rafting 160 miles down the Alatna River. This feat was made all the more remarkable because he supplemented an organic diet with natural edibles. Like many young people seeking physical challenges and spiritual meaning, David Brill walked the length of the Appalachian Trail. In *As Far As the Eye Can See*, Brill reflects on the joys and personal growth of solitary walking as well as the poignant moments of social intercourse at camps along the 2,100 miles from Georgia to Maine. Similarly, Chris Townsend replayed the personal challenges of trekking 900 miles along the Canadian Rockies. He shares impressive tales of endurance and personal reflection as a solo hiker in *High Summer*.

Unquestionably, solo walks, hikes, treks, rafting, biking, or other forms of wilderness travel provide unusual opportunities for intimate connections with nature and impressive personal growth. Bruce Barcott describes the benefits after years of hiking solo at Mount Rainier: "There is something extraordinary about being alone on a mountain. Vulnerability sharpens every sense. Fear visits the body with a physical coldness. Moments of bliss are intensified and made melancholy by the realization that the moment will be yours alone and never shared. Only solo do you understand the indiscriminate power of the mountain and feel to your humble bones the insignificance of a human voice raised upon it." Aloneness provides incredibly rich moments of insight and individual development for those who venture out into the wilderness.

A closer inspection of the adventure stories described above suggests that solitude and aloneness are often counterbalanced by purposeful pursuit of social interaction. Once you get past the surface of these tales, it is apparent that the adventurers also craved company. Barcott was slogging through freezing mist and rain on his way to Golden Lakes at Mount Rainier. It being September, few other hikers were on the trail, and Barcott began to fear for his safety given the initial signs of hypothermia. He makes a turn in the trail and suddenly comes upon two other hikers and blurts out: "Oh thank God! People! I love you!" Within minutes he was sitting in the ranger's cabin at

Golden Lakes and hardly containing his glee at being with other people. What then unfolds is a hilarious reminiscence of enjoying the company of others there in the windy, freezing, wet wilderness.

David Brill's tales about daily life hiking the Appalachian Trail inevitably replay the complex socialization process that nurtures and supports individual efforts to overcome the physical, mental, spiritual, and emotional challenges of the trail. Thru-hikers adopt personal monikers and routinely join, quit, and rejoin small groups of other hikers. For everyone except the truly oddball or crass individual, the society of thru-hikers looks after its own through selfless sharing, exhortation, and camaraderie.

Edward Abbey writes in a most eloquent fashion about desert wildness and the glory of being alone in *Desert Solitaire*. He also shares his passion for routinely visiting nearby towns for social entertainment at the local bars. Similarly, at the end of walking the length of the Grand Canyon, Colin Fletcher found that his last day was not as inspiring as he thought it would be. He notes, "The world is not, unfortunately, all beauty or all grandeur. And what I needed now, as a corrective, was some ugliness and some pettiness. I would drive home, I decided, through Las Vegas."

We all crave solitude when the pressure and impact of urban life become excessive. Most of us have the romantic notion that venturing to the wilderness alone is the ideal prescription to set us straight. However, in my experience wilderness adventures are better when they involve both solitude and other people. In fact, sharing wildness inevitably builds strong bonds of friendship and community. Without community we cannot have culture; and without community we cannot build a culture that loves the earth.

It was a pretty despicable lot huddled around the campfire. In the backcountry for four days, we looked, smelled, and talked like mountain dwellers. Along about the third day in the wilderness, you begin to lose that need for purity and obsession with remaining completely clean. A simple act of washing your hands feels like having just bathed from head to toe. Washing your hair and face is tantamount to total cleanliness. Heating hot water after breakfast and cleaning my hair is now a favorite ritual. No matter how cold it is, you feel so refreshed that it is worth any agony to perform this act. A quart of warm water and you are all set to go. Refreshing. Invigorating. Friends often want desperately to clean up after a long night, but they just cannot get over the inertia created by that chilly morning breeze. They slink around camp until one frantically asks, "Is there enough hot water for me too?"

An interesting transformation occurs twenty-four hours into the wild. Without the normal visual cues provided in society—hyperclean bodies conveyed through television, billboard, and radio advertising— you can easily begin to regress toward a more natural state of existence. That is, in part, why many seek the wild. There are solid reasons why hypercleanliness is critical in teeming populations without much personal space. When huddling cheek by jowl in an elevator with limited air circulation, community cleanliness takes on heightened significance. Different perfumes and odors from personal hygiene products attain valuable relevance. Outdoors, these same scents can bring on undesired consequences when bees, bears, or other critters fall in love with your armpits.

Charlie, Dick, Bill, Don, and I did not have to worry about olfactory insults that afternoon standing there in the smoke of a small blaze. After four days of morning and evening campfires in the Weminuche Wilderness of southern Colorado, the only thing we could smell was smoke. Happy hour had begun following a day of hiking and the group was in a mellow mood. Dick brought out a can of smoked clams. Bill offered up salsa and chips. Don provided a few nuts. Charlie managed to find some crackers and cheese in his pack. I pulled out carrot sticks and ranch salad dressing. The communal table was set. Several shared wine, while others sipped bourbon. Our mood was festive and relaxing. Stories had begun and Dick was regaling us with a tale of another futile elk-hunting trip that involved extricating his vehicle from a snow bank, sliding around icy curves with chains on all four wheels, and waiting in below-zero temperatures only to see nothing. Each contemplated the lies they would foist on the group next, lies that grow proportionately to the spirits consumed.

Charlie pulled off his baseball cap while Dick told about elk prints as big as moose hoofs. A startlingly greasy mess of hair flopped out in the midst of this exercise—not good form, Charlie. Don was standing there with clam bits and clam juice dribbling off his beard, oblivious to the fact. Bill unzipped his parka as the fire grew hot. Beneath the parka was the sorriest looking polypropylene thermal underwear—how could you possibly get that much dirt on your shirt, Bill? I bent down to tie my shoe and looked at my ridiculous combination of blue long underwear as a background against faded purple shorts. If a "dork look" was marketable, I was wearing a winning combination that would make me a millionaire. I straightened up and looked at Dick's hands caressing his plastic cup of libations—black grease highlighted his fingernails. We were a sad-looking but mellowing community unfettered by society's expectations. That was all to change in an instant without any forewarning.

Up the trail walked what at that moment was the most beautiful woman on earth. Young and fetching in her fly-fishing ensemble, she captured everyone's attention. It was suddenly silent, and my compatriots just stood there with food falling out of their mouths. She had on the right waders with the right felt-soled fishing boots, complimented by a blowzy long-sleeved shirt with rolled sleeves. Her long auburn hair was pulled back in a ponytail. She balanced a rod delicately in her hand as she picked her way along the trail. And, to her great discretion, she did not acknowledge that we were there. The dark thoughts were about to roll off the tongues of my colleagues when a few seconds behind her came a sugar daddy. Older than her, but displaying a relationship that shouted, "No, she's not my daughter," he continued to walk up the trail. Then the comments flowed profusely.

Suddenly we all felt very grungy and miserable. We were whisked in those few seconds back to civilization and all the wonderful things that it has to offer. "Damn shame she isn't with a real man like me," said one of the filthy five. "Looked like they stepped out of an Orvis catalog," said another. "Those are just day people," replied a third, implying that they could not meet the test that we had plunged ourselves into the last four days. "I want to go home," sang a fourth. I turned around and continued preparing for dinner.

Walking to the fringe of trees in which we had camped to drain water from rice, I could see them down at Squaw Creek with their sensuous fly-casting motions seeking to kill fish. The gentleman was a picture of fly-casting perfection. He wore a silly, floppy cap with a few flies in it beneath the world's ugliest sunglasses. He had on the requisite red flannel shirt and all of the proper accouterments outdoor retailers claim are essential for catching the big ones. Both of them showed grace in their casting—they were definitely not novices at this. I felt like I was a voyeur looking down on something illicit. Damn, it had been a good trip to this point. Hate to see it all go downhill just because of two people intent on displaying their finery.

The Magic of the Weminuche

For the next half hour we finished our hors d'oeuvres and hugged libations close to our chests. There was still some comfort by that smoky campfire after all. Dick launched into yet another tale of hiking the Grand Canyon, transporting us to the mammoth valley and remembrances of trips past, a radical difference from the greenery, water, and snow of the Weminuche Wilderness. Don finished cooking trout caught farther up Squaw Creek and added them to the rice and canned chicken. Wilted salad was distributed, and we applied dressing. It was a typical starvation meal without much in the way of fine touches, but then this was the last night of the trip. You really could not expect much better.

As I shoveled the first bite into my mouth, the consummate fishing couple walked by, headed downstream. History repeated itself. We just stood there with our mouths open without saying a word. They did not grace our presence with so much as a glance. At that moment I foresaw the evening before them.

They would stroll back to the lodge by the trailhead and shower before going to the lodge's sitting room for just the right gin and tonic. Refreshed by their exercise and clean to the bone, they would have gourmet hors d'oeuvres prepared by the lodge's renowned chef. This would just be the prelude. Waiting was filet mignon and fresh trout (not caught by the couple—they only played at fishing, and besides, Don had already fished out the stream) along with long-grain wild rice grown by the Utes, a local Indian tribe. The sommelier had selected the proper wine to bring out the best flavors in the entree. Dessert would be a delicate chocolate mousse. Then, despite the protestations of other lodge guests who wanted to savor their intelligent, witty, and worldly conversation, the couple would slip off to their cabin for the real exercise of the day.

Within seconds they passed. It took more than a couple of logs to revive the campfire and our spirits. Of course, no one wanted to admit that they would rather be headed for that same destination—warm, dry lodge, hot shower, gourmet food, beauty, passion, and deep sleep. However, a pro could read the thoughts simply in the absence of conversation. Dishes were washed. Don scrubbed out the frying pan. Cigars were lit and proper hot chocolate was made with just the right touch of bourbon. Darkness began to close on the filthy five huddled there in the copse of evergreens. The fire flamed as Charlie rearranged the logs, and then Dick launched into a tale of the time he almost drowned on the Penobscot River while canoeing. Hell, he almost drowned on Vallecito Creek outside of Durango while canoeing. Remind me not to share a canoe with him.

The Weminuche Wilderness is not easy to reach from any major city outside of Albuquerque, even then a three-hour drive away, and this fact was the reason I came to live in the high desert. Most Denver folk never get past the Collegiate Peaks. I've found that I typically share it with people off the plains—who have difficulty functioning at the high altitude—or the passionately dedicated.

I first read about the Weminuche Wilderness in Dennis Gebhardt's now infamous *A Backpacking Guide to the Weminuche Wilderness*. Gebhardt can hardly be blamed for writing a guide to this formerly pristine country. He did so back in the mid-1970s at the tail end of the outdoors craze. In the late 1990s and early 2000s there has been a return to the outdoors, but in a new, redefined way. Extreme sports and experiences dominate the contemporary outdoor quest—the emphasis being on action, adventure, and grueling contests (for example, the Eco-Challenge). This has left the wilderness to the few who are willing to forgo their cell phones and lattés.

Gebhardt's guide is startling. He argues that he never built a campfire in the eight hundred miles of hiking needed to write his book. He also claims that he carried only a heavy wool shirt for insulation. Either he had one heck of a down sleeping bag, or he was seriously abnormal in terms of metabolism, because the Weminuche Wilderness can be absolutely frigid, with elevations well above ten thousand feet. Gebhardt's guide was written at a time when all authorities had concluded that the grizzly bear was extinct in Colorado. Gebhardt hypothesized that there were still some pockets of the wilderness in which the great bear roamed. Sitting on the Continental Divide, looking down into the Beaver Creek or Goose Creek drainages, very wild country, gives Gebhardt's hypothesis weight—and only three years after Gebhardt published his guide, a bow hunter exterminated the "last" grizzly in the Weminuche Wilderness.

There still is speculation that the grizzly roams the South San Juan Wilderness, just over the border from New Mexico. The Round River group, encouraged by Doug Peacock, Rick Bass, and David Petersen, has been unable to provide conclusive documentation that the great bear travels these mountains. Let's agree that it does and then close the wilderness to any sort of intrusion. That would take care of the matter.

The Magic of the Weminuche

A great opportunity lies here within our grasp. For those who don't want to assume that the grizzly exists in the San Juans, ship down a few and close the forest. Leave them alone, and they will thrive.

Gebhardt's guide describes an intriguing river valley that ends at the Continental Divide. The Squaw Creek trail sounds like a great place to visit, as the elevation gain is gradual up to the divide. Be forewarned that it also has a sheep/stock drive in the valley (this is true); that it retains very cold air throughout the summer (this is true); that it has hordes of flies and horseflies (this is true); that it takes forever to reach on lousy roads (this is true); that the trail up the valley is often obscured by runoff, ponds, and marshes (this is true); and that wild beasts prowl this valley (this is true). Come to think of it, there are many other better places to visit in the Weminuche.

The trailhead at 9,400 feet is high country in which to start any trip. A stiff climb of several hundred feet brings you to a well-constructed bridge across Squaw Creek. Pure waters flow, swirl, and babble among rocks before cascading through a narrowing of the valley. The waterway can be a major torrent depending on the time of the season and the amount of snowfall. There are enough holes in the forest canopy for the sun to shine and sparkle on this lovely stream. In many respects, Squaw Creek is unique for its tranquility and crystal-clear flow. But, in truth, it is just like so many other beautiful Colorado streams that are even more accessible.

The trail climbs above the stream and valley narrows to avoid a precipitous drop-off—the result of past geological movements. Above and removed from the water now, the trail continues to ascend through rocky scree slopes and soft aspen glades for about one mile. Then it levels off and makes a beeline up the valley toward the creek. The view toward the Continental Divide suggests high, lonesome country with few visitors. Lush patches of tall purple lupine grow among the aspens and add color to the green glades. This classic Colorado scene is framed from the trail—tall green aspens parting for a glimpse of the divide, vivid flower gardens among the cool forest, sparkling stream in the valley gurgling downward.

Visits to Squaw Creek were so enjoyable that I asked my friend Dick to come down from Colorado Springs to spend some time there. He brought along his son, Ryan, who was not at all certain that he wanted to be there away from his buddies. Although the trail was open, the mountains and plateau around Squaw Creek were still covered with snow. However, daytime temperatures were in the mid-eighties. All seemed right.

We made good time to our usual campsite and then considered which trail to take for the afternoon. The last trip I had walked up to Squaw Lake, which is in the subalpine zone, but barely. Towering above Squaw Lake is the final climb through tundra to the Divide. A beautiful high lake in a cold and desolate basin, softened on the south by spruce trees, Squaw Lake would still be under ice at this point. We opted for the climb over Squaw Peak, recognizing that we would never make the top owing to the lingering snow.

Ry led the way up the stock driveway. Few people in their right mind walk this path for good reason. It takes a direct line up the mountain to reach the valley on the other side. Thus, there really is no constructed tread or switchbacks, only scrambling up one hillock, over a group of rocks, or through an aspen forest of matchsticks to make progress difficult. This is high country, so the effect is much worse if you are not acclimated. We marked our passage toward the snowline by looking at the ridge across Squaw Creek. It would be much higher on this sunny slope, until the approaching thick timber of the spruce and fir forest would block further progress.

Signs of sheepherders littered the trail. Larger aspens bore carvings of names and dates. Rusted cans were strewn along the way. Perhaps the herders just ejected any weight they could when they climbed these hills. The trail confirmed what rugged and independent people are needed to herd stock or sheep.

Returning to camp, we took a few breaks to gaze out on the snowy northern San Juan Range. Looking over this vast countryside, I found it easy to understand why the Weminuche was the last stronghold of the grizzly in Colorado. Many of these trails and driveways cut through country that seldom sees visitors. The grizzly must be able to exist without detection in plenty of the drainages. However, the search for survivors has turned to the South San Juan Wilderness, where huge private landholdings may inadvertently have formed grizzly refuges.

Lengthening shadows of the spruces warned that it was time to begin dinner. Despite valiant efforts, a blazing fire never materialized. In part, the problem was finding dry wood. Too much of the available wood under the trees had not dried out from the past winter. The fire sort of sputtered its way along while emitting vast volumes of smoke. Cooking an Italian dish, we tossed burnable garbage into the fire for fuel.

The Magic of the Weminuche

As darkness settled over the camp, our merry blaze reflected light off the trees. It was going to be colder than we anticipated because of the heavy snow cover. We hugged the fire and told riotous tales. It was comforting to have the companionship of friends and fire. There in the warmth of the yellow flickering blaze I once again came to know why Dick is such a good friend. Ry began to share his thoughts on the future of his young life. The bonds of friendship and community deepened.

Without much moonlight to brighten our camp, the steel-blue stars began to twinkle brightly in the frigid air; I was certainly happy to have brought the heavy-duty sleeping bag rated to -5 degrees. Would it be enough? Retiring to our respective tents, I zipped the front door up most of the way to block the silent movement of cold air down from the mountain and drifted off to sleep.

It was about 2:00 a.m. when the first sound woke me with a start. It was a bit like a baby crying. It took several minutes to wake up and become alert. I listened intently. "No sound now. I must have been dreaming." Then the sound rose again. This time a branch snapped sharply, there was a slight thud, and then a wailing sound in close proximity of our camp. All of a sudden it was terribly clear—"That's the bawl of a bear cub." The bawling continued as it circled the camp. What to do? I had kept a package of peanuts in the tent for the early morning and caloric replenishment. That now seemed like a mistake of the worst magnitude. "Should I open the tent and shine my flashlight to see what's out there? Should I call out to Dick and Ry?"

The tent walls seemed mighty thin at that very moment. Extricating a pocketknife from the first aid kit in case it was necessary to cut my way out of the tent, I unzipped my bag so that I would not be trapped. And with the bawling trailing off, an extremely bad ten minutes in the backcountry came to an end. Shivering from the cold and excitement, I decided it was time to jettison the peanuts. The last thing I wanted was a bear looking for food in the tent. I quickly opened the door, stepped out, and threw the peanuts for all they were worth down toward Squaw Creek. I did not want the bears to associate the peanuts with the lump of warm meat sleeping in the dark blue cocoon of feathers and nylon.

Dick and Ry slept through the whole thing. I looked for tracks in the morning, but could not find anything. It may have been a cub that was trying to reach our food that we had properly hung for protection. Perhaps the cub fell off in its climb to reach the food. We added to our problem by cooking aromatic food and then throwing garbage and leftovers in the fire to burn. Some of the food must not have burned thoroughly, for the fire had continued to send delicious scents into the air. The aromatic smoke phenomenon is credited with creating criminal bears in Yosemite Valley. Almost one thousand campfires or barbecues are lit every night in Yosemite. Smoke sends powerful messages to bruins that cannot resist temptation. Here at Squaw Creek it was still very early in the season, and the latent snow pack may have prevented food sources from maturing.

This was the scariest night I had ever spent in the wilderness. It was one very long time from 2:00 a.m. until light began to show at 5:00 a.m. I was up early and tried to get the fire going. Once out of the bag I found out just how cold it was. We had burned most of the wood from the previous night, so I went back to my bag. After 6:00 a.m., Dick finally arose. He was startled to hear that there was a bear in the camp, but he was more startled by the gift of heavy frost that covered everything. It was a classic Colorado morning after a frigid night.

We decided that breakfast would taste much better down at the truck in the sunlight. Another good hour and a half remained before the sun would shine generously on our camp, and there was not enough wood left to keep warm for that long. Hustling along the trail, we finally built up enough heat to be comfortable. But the evidence of the hard freeze was everywhere. Isolated small pools on Squaw Creek had a glazed sheet of ice over them. All grass and flowers in the meadows were covered in frosty rime. In the shade the world glowed with an icy brilliance while over on the sunny slope west of Squaw Creek, the earth warmed to a new day and progression toward summer. Dick, Ry, and I warmed to the friendship of our tightly knit community.

Community can be found in another person or companion. While most of my treks to the Weminuche Wilderness involve three or more people, occasionally only one person is able to free up the time to enjoy wilderness. But the same sense of community forms rapidly in conversation and caring for tasks associated with living together in the wild.

In the Pine River valley of the Weminuche Wilderness, I was on the verge of becoming a rescue victim. It all started so innocently enough, and I learned a significant lesson about how people unwittingly spiral toward calamity. In the end, community prevailed. The Pine River trailhead begins at an elevation of 7,900 feet. The trail winds for twenty-two miles up a drainage to Weminuche Pass and from there the trail continues down to Squaw Creek.

The Magic of the Weminuche

On a mid-June morning, my friend Terrye and I drove her Toyota Land Cruiser up Highway 550 toward Cuba, New Mexico. Terrye is one of the world's best mountaineers. She scales mountains as if it were child's play. Her strength of character ensures she will achieve whatever peak she sets out to climb. If stranded on top of a peak and needing assistance, Terrye would be the one to fight blizzard and storm to get to you. In addition, she keeps herself in tremendous shape at all times. We never, ever, let Terrye lead on a trail if we want to enjoy a hike.

After Bayfield, Colorado, we turned off the state highway while taking the back road to Vallecito Lake and the trailhead for the Pine River. Crossing over the Los Pinos River at the highway, Terrye was beginning to get edgy after riding for so long. I had to remember not to let her get in the lead. Near the reservoir we rounded a bend, and there in the middle of the road were hundreds of sheep with a shepherd and dogs busily at work. We had to nudge our way into the crowd in order to get by.

We circled Vallecito Lake, mobbed with boaters at the height of the season. The campgrounds were packed trailer-to-trailer. As we slowly navigated the circumference of Vallecito Lake, all we could see were people—people in cars, people in boats, people on horseback, people on foot, people on bikes, people on all-terrain vehicles, people, people, people. It was time to reach the trailhead.

By the time we shouldered our packs, it was very warm for the Weminuche at this time of year—in the low eighties. But having just traveled from the low nineties of New Mexico, we thought that the temperature felt pretty good. We had been hiking in much hotter weather for more than a month by this point. The trail is shaded in many spots and follows the Pine River, so that water is normally available. Still, it was refreshing to enter the shade of the huge ponderosa pines that line the trail.

Looking up river was a sight that had become a signature portrait. Granite Peak stood out massively to the east on our right, and Runlett Peak dominated the view to the left. Both peaks guard the entrance to the valley. We would parallel Granite Peak Ranch. With miles of green meadows leading into a mixed forest of aspen, pine, and fir, someone is a lucky beneficiary of this wild acreage. Down by the river is a small settlement of rustic buildings—a lodge and outbuildings. Walking along the fence of Granite Peak Ranch, I could think only about how healthy it would be to spend an entire summer at this serene ranch.

Six

We walked the pine needle–covered trail, alternating between two ruts that form the trail. The needles resonated that inviting pine scent, reminding us all of the forest. Warm sun had conspired with the pines to produce a heavenly elixir. Terrye somehow managed to take the lead and I held back. She was unwinding. From the rear I watched her clenched fists slowly begin to open and after two miles her hands were loose at her sides without tightly balled fists. The Pine was working its magic.

We passed merry Indian Creek, splashing happily down from the high country. Terrye turned around with a big smile on her face. She was nearing her zone of happiness. Most of the first four miles pass peacefully with little strain once you leave Indian Creek because the trail gains modest elevation as it parallels the Pine River. Our destination was six miles to the confluence of Emerald Creek, which falls from Emerald Lake. Many camps along the river beckon, but the key is to plod along until you reach the spot where the two streams meet.

The Pine River trail is always interesting. One minute you are scooting through a stand of aspen, and the next quarter-mile you are negotiating around a rockslide and stopping to look up to see where the scree fell from on Runlett Peak. You must be vigilant for Rocky Mountain bighorn sheep. They are drawn down to the valley by the lush vegetation. The way meanders among a leafy green cottonwood and willow forest on the flood plain of the Pine. Tall pines and firs frame the sides of the valley. At spots you break out into the bright sun and marvel at impossibly green meadows occupying the benches above the river.

Our walk was so pleasant that we did not stop once on the way to the campsite. However, after five miles of steady walking with a loaded pack, we both were hungry and thirsty—but, having gained only four hundred feet in reaching this point, only a little tired. In a grassy meadow under huge cottonwood trees, we each began to erect our colorful nylon tents. I was also looking for a spot that would warm up first thing in the morning because the cold air drains off the stratospheric San Juans and settles overnight in the river valleys.

Our afternoon would be spent hiking up to Emerald Lake. Finishing a baloney sandwich and taking a few slugs of water, I indicated to Terrye that I was ready to go. I emptied my backpack and placed essential survival gear inside for the trip up to 10,033 feet and Emerald Lake, which is attained after a climb of 2,600 feet. At Emerald Lake, the valley opens onto peaks in the 12,500-foot range. This is only the appetizer. The series of 12,500-foot peaks blend into 13,000-foot and higher peaks up in Moon Lake Basin.

Terrye was magnetically drawn to these sentinels and prodded me onward. The day had turned truly warm by this point and I felt a lassitude that I interpreted as lack of sleep. It's a long hard trip to the trailhead, and then an easy but several-hour walk to Emerald Lake trail junction. I really wanted to just sit down and relax. Terrye led the way.

The trail slipped in and out of the sun, which beat down unforgivingly on the mountainside. Down low at the trail junction, the mixed forest of pine, aspen, and cottonwood provided shady shelter. The trail had a few switchbacks in climbing the first six hundred feet, but then it reduced to a steep uphill climb along Lake Creek. The way was very hot and dry above the creek, and we were seldom in a position to obtain water easily.

We entered into a boggy meadow rife with skunk cabbage. This green clearing hinted at sources of water working down from higher unnamed peaks above. Where else but in Colorado would you have a succession of 12,282-, 12,284-, 12,275-, and 12,495-foot peaks that are regarded as just another long ridge?

When the trail intersected Lake Creek with its sparkling waters prancing merrily down the mountain, I was beginning to feel very tired and lethargic. We were really getting within range, though, and it was crazy to think about stopping now.

The trail entered a large rock and snow slide area, with small aspens the only trees. In the hottest part of the day, we slogged across the rock face. The tantalizing shade of the forest lay ahead, along with a series of switchbacks that would take us into the basin of Little Emerald Lake and Emerald Lake.

Entering the shade, I told Terrye that I had to stop and refuel. Reaching for my canteen and an old trusty Snickers Bar for replenishment, I took several long drinks of water. I felt somewhat light-headed, which I attributed to being at ten thousand feet. I just could not get my energy level up and I thought about turning back, but I knew that Terrye really wanted to see the lake. After all, we had come this far, and it was just a half-mile away. I forced myself to continue on the death march. We topped the rise on the rock fall that forms the natural dam for Emerald Lake and began a slight descent around Little Emerald Lake.

By this time I was really laboring, nauseated and light-headed in a way I had never felt before. We came to the shores of Emerald Lake, and I told Terrye this was absolutely enough. I was shaken. I honestly did not think that I could make it back to camp, and I grew very apprehensive. I was trying to sweat profusely but did not seem to have the fluids to do so—this was similar to initial stages of shock. Here I was ten miles into the wilderness with virtually no one around, and I was losing it. Given her diminutive size, I could not rely on Terrye to drag me out of here, and I did not like the prospects of being here alone while she went for help. I put myself in this predicament; I should get myself out of it.

Terrye, bless her heart, snapped to attention. While I pulled out a sandwich, thinking I might be hungry, Terrye filled her now-empty quart bottle with lake water, keeping out debris as best she could, and adding a packet of sport drink mix. I downed it in a few gulps.

We started down immediately, but it was a very shaky walk for the next two miles. The toughest part was the sixty feet out of the lake's basin. Once I was going downhill, my confidence returned. The fluids had begun to take effect. About halfway down at the nine-thousand-foot level I began to feel somewhat normal. This had been a big scare. Ready to reach camp, I was tired, hot, and eager to be off my sore feet. Never did a camp look so good as when we dropped off the trail. Immediately I began filtering water to rehydrate my body.

I took off my favorite boots—boots that had seen hundreds upon hundreds of miles. The bottoms of both my feet were covered in blisters. As I slipped on my running shoes, I exclaimed as much to Terrye. She, too, was pulling off her boots and found that she had the same affliction. Six miles had to be covered to get back to the car. That would certainly be no fun whatsoever.

The night passed very slowly. Combined heat exhaustion and altitude sickness kept my spirits down. Terrye was also melancholy. She too must have been suffering from mild heat exhaustion. We ate an unremarkable meal and shuffled around camp that night.

Morning arrived crisp and clear. We both wanted to be out to the car before it even hinted of being hot. Despite this motivation, we would be walking very gingerly for six miles, and the prospects were not encouraging. Onto the trail we hobbled and worked into our rhythm. It was a half-mile down the trail when the beauty of the morning grabbed hold of me. The air was cool, but not cold. The light was at its best—not harsh, but warm and glowing. The trees retained a radiance that I probably otherwise would not have noticed. The Pine River silently, strongly, and swiftly made its way down the valley. And then it all came into perspective for me.

Although I was physically challenged this morning, the Pine River and its companions—the rocks, peaks, trees, waterfalls—had not changed. They would be the same this morning and the next in their radiant existence. To be certain, they would change—a rock would fall here, a tree would die and decay there, flowers would blossom, a beaver would take several fish for a meal, the wind would blow dust from hundreds of miles away onto the snow pack at Buffalo Peak, a creek would begin to form a new channel, and thousands of other minute, but important, alterations would occur. Still, in human eyes, the Pine River would be the same. We needed to look at our situation with the same perspective. Yes, we were exiting a little beaten and bowed. We would recover and would learn lessons that help us appreciate the magic of these magnificent mountains.

Nature has a remarkable ability to pull people together. In past centuries, wilderness was seen as a threat, which in turn created a strong motivation for building and maintaining communities. Today nature has restorative power and is valued for its healing potential. It can provide a context in which human community is strengthened.

The Squaw Creek camp shared with Dick, Don, Bill, and Charlie provided a venue for rebuilding a community of friends. Although each individual was responsible for a breakfast or dinner, all chipped in with various food and libations at happy hour. Each of us assumed certain camp responsibilities spontaneously—hanging food, gathering firewood, washing dishes, or purifying water. Nonetheless, the sum of our voluntary contributions blended into a community of action. As we look back on the experience, we find that wilderness brought us together. We endured the hard, cold, dirty ground at night. The drizzly, frigid morning we departed was spent around a meager fire with little warmth—all of us felt the same modest hardship. On day trips we marveled at perfectly constructed beaver dams, dense stands of beautiful blue spruce, and soft green marshes bursting with tiny flowers.

A subsequent camp at Squaw Creek with Dick and Ry forged a different type of community. There in the wild mountains of Colorado, on trail or around the fire, we discussed the problems confronting us, venting frustrations, seeking solace, and looking for advice. Ryan ruminated about his plans on attending college—if, where, and when. Dick considered his bittersweet experience with his deanship at the university while pondering when the right time would be to exit. I sought validation for a new truck I was thinking of purchasing. It would be impossible to look back at that camp and not remember the care and concern we showed for each other—a community of support.

The adventure with Terrye to Emerald Lake surfaced another aspect of community that frequently occurs in wild areas. Struggling against difficult circumstances, we formed a small community to extricate ourselves from harm's way. Neither of us will ever forget the strength of the sun, the dryness and heat that conspired to rob us of our abilities, or the compassion that we gave to each other in hobbling back to the trailhead.

Adventures in nature provide a context in which people build strong relations. A common experience, whether the thankful appreciation of soft summer morning or impressive thunderous rainstorm, bonds people together in a community. These relations are essential for building an earth-based culture, a culture in which people, as one, simply love the earth and its wildness.

La querencia—Sandia Mountains, New Mexico.

South Peak, Sandia Mountain Wilderness, New Mexico.

Early morning Pine River, Weminuche Wilderness, Colorado.

Aspen grove, Weminuche Wilderness, Colorado.

Beckoning high country, Weminuche Wilderness, Colorado.

Emerald Lake, Weminuche Wilderness, Colorado.

*Squaw Creek, Weminuche
Wilderness, Colorado.*

*Squaw Creek Trail,
Weminuche
Wilderness,
Colorado.*

Crossing the West Fork of the Gila River, Gila Wilderness, New Mexico.

Middle Fork of the Gila River,
Gila Wilderness, New Mexico.

Hoodoos, Gila Wilderness,
New Mexico.

Big Meadows, Gila Wilderness, New Mexico.

Carbon Glacier, Mount Rainier National Park, Washington.

Cataract Creek, Mount Rainier National Park, Washington.

Mystic Lake below Willis Wall, Mount Rainier National Park, Washington.

Snow-covered trail to Summerland, Mount Rainier National Park, Washington.

The Gila Wilderness

7

One of life's great joys is a long trip deep into wilderness, disengaged from the intrusions of technology and immersed in a spellbinding natural environment. Every person should have an opportunity to make such a journey at least once in life. Not only would this build a deep appreciation for the wild, but it would also help others to form a better understanding of the value underlying community. Cut off from the comforts of home; freed from the computer, television, radio, or CD player; unable to shower or bathe easily; reliant on others to assist in the fundamental tasks of purifying water, gathering firewood, and preparing meals; and bound together in the interests of safety, you find that it does not take very long to forge strong bonds with fellow travelers. You develop a sense of community, an almost forgotten thread of American society.

C. L. Rawlins roamed the northern Rocky Mountains as a backcountry hydrologist, monitoring the insidious effects of civilization on the purity of snow, rain, and water in high mountain lakes. In *Sky's Witness*, Rawlins describes many trips with other scientists into desolate wilderness areas, most often undertaken in winter with very harsh weather. Rawlins's tales provide great delight about the raw beauty of skiing through subzero temperatures with mind-numbing wind-chill; exhalations of frosty clouds from deep breathing under hundred-pound packs; snow-draped conifers; powdery trails requiring enormous effort to make progress; and extreme living at the edge, miles from human assistance.

Most of Rawlins's trips occur when days are very short and blessed sunlight is a brief visitor. Consequently, he spends vast amounts of time with companions in small, cramped tents and frigid, rough-hewn cabins in the middle of nowhere. Rawlins carefully analyzes each of his companions and ruminates about their strengths and liabilities for these trips. One can be very taciturn and temperamental, but the absolute best to have around when conditions deteriorate in a life-threatening situation. Another is introspective and much easier to live with when the weather is mellow. A third withdraws when he is uneasy and grows distant as challenges present themselves.

Despite differences in personality and mix of companions on these backcountry sojourns, Rawlins always uplifts the bonds of sharing—the community of friends—as an essential ingredient for survival and a desired instrumentality for enjoying wildness. The longer the trip, the deeper into the wilderness, and the more hazardous the situations, the more rewarding are the gifts of community. Wildness, therefore, can contribute to deeply enriched relations among people and a sense of togetherness that is being lost in urban society. A culture that loves the earth will benefit from and build upon community among those who treasure the wild.

We dropped down from the lofty Mogollon Rim in northern Arizona, the rush of wind the only sound disturbing an otherwise tranquil afternoon. The sweet smell of pine flooded the car and confirmed that a new season had begun in the high country. The warm sun gently baked the world's largest ponderosa pine forest. Sap was gradually flowing within the giant trees. Life began to dance to the penetrating light in celebration of bitter days past. Outside all of nature came poignantly alive through sharp scents, busy buzzing insects, chirping birds, greening shrubs and trees, colorful flowers and soft breezes. It was good to be alive.

Although the temperature at this seven-thousand-foot elevation might have been idyllic, there was only one way for it to go, and that was up. Several hours of driving would bring me to the home of my friend Jim and the launching point for a multi-day excursion through New Mexico's Gila Wilderness.

Wading into the stifling heat of the Verde River, I turned my thoughts to the coming week and the circuit we intended to make up the West Fork of the Gila River, across a high plateau, and then down the Middle Fork. Here, at the end of May, the Forest Service records indicated that the average temperature peaked in the high eighties with a low in the fifties. Coming from Flagstaff, where highs typically reached the low to mid-seventies and the high thirties at night, I was most concerned about being too hot. Consequently, my pack was definitely on the light side.

The first stop would be in Phoenix at the Holubar store. Once famous for high-quality, featherweight equipment, Holubar made a very lightweight sleeping bag rated to plus fifteen degrees. The bag had 60-percent fill on top to maximize its efficiency. Looking at the long trek in the Gila with substantially higher temperatures than Flagstaff, I thought it only natural to shed pounds. The sales associate had disappointing news, indicating that they did not have any fifteen-degree bags with a right-hand zipper in stock. This was definitely not good, but also not a problem. I had brought an "elephant's foot" as a backup. An elephant's foot is a bivouac bag that covers approximately two-thirds of your body. A thick down coat would complement the bag and ensure sound sleep. I caught the surface streets back to the freeway.

That night was spent with Jim and his father, Bill, down in Tucson. We shared an excellent, hyperhot chile meal at a dumpy-looking Mexican restaurant, anticipating food depravation on the long trip. At dinner talk turned to the others that would be joining us. Tim, an avid birder, was intent on expanding his life list. He was a slim fellow and in excellent shape from his many outdoors excursions seeking elusive avian trophies. Also joining us on the trip was Claus, a stout fellow who knew and loved the mountains. This would be our community of comrades.

Into the Gila (Day One)

The next morning we squeezed into Jim's Bronco and headed toward the Gila after dividing up food, cooking equipment, and tents. It would take the better part of the day to drive east into New Mexico and then up toward Silver City. From Silver City the road enters the piñon, juniper, and pine forests and rough, precipitous canyons. It is a long, slow, and torturous drive to the Gila Hot Springs. I was very happy to reach the grade leading steeply down toward the visitor center and cliff dwellings.

The Gila Wilderness became America's first designated National Forest Wilderness in 1924, but it was not until 1964 that Congress established the official wilderness system. The Gila earned renown from the famed naturalist Aldo Leopold, and from the centrality of the wilderness in the development of Arizona and New Mexico. The mountains of the Mogollon, Diablo, Tularosa, and Black ranges possess a vivid history. By the late 1870s there had been many attempts at prospecting, homesteading, and ranching them. Clashes with Indians threatened those trying to domesticate the Gila. Today, Gila country includes vast wild areas coexisting side-by-side with important local communities.

The Gila possesses four of the six life zones that the ecologist C. Hart Merriam identified in the nineteenth century, life zones that range from low desert to neoarctic, and on a lengthy backcountry trip it is not unusual to experience several, if not all, of them. Dominant vegetation along streams includes cottonwoods, box elders, and locust. Shaded and higher elevations find spruce, fir, and aspen. Open mountain areas have scattered cover of piñon, pine, and juniper. Elevations range from roughly five thousand feet to almost eleven thousand feet. Life revolves around the narrow canyons where reliable water is found.

At the Gila Hot Springs, the road levels out and curves dissipate. The valley, though at nearly six thousand feet, is generally quite warm. We stopped at the visitor center to fill our water bottles and inquire about trail conditions. It was still too early in the season for much news to have made its way back to the deskbound rangers. Most people just leave after finishing a major hike and do not share information about trail conditions with them, so the news they receive is often spotty and not up to date. From the scant reports, it appeared that the Gila was experiencing normal water flows—an important consideration since much of the trail was across, in, and around the river.

Parking at the road's end by the cliff dwellings, we shouldered our packs. The temperature was in the mid-eighties, and thus quite comfortable on the shady sections of the trail. I was especially glad for this warmth in view of my sleeping equipment. A trail sign indicated the way to several of our destinations—Hells Hole was a bit over twelve miles and White Creek sixteen miles from our vehicle. Although we did not have any specific target for each day, we did plan on averaging about six miles per day in order to complete the loop. There, among the box elder, locust, New Mexico privet, and scrawny pine, we took our first steps on the sandy trail.

Soon the shade ran out and we were walking through the sandy canyon bottom. Hills rose gradually on each side, sparsely covered in juniper, some piñon, and some pine. Deciduous trees spread out along the canyon bottom, the most prevalent being varieties of cottonwoods. Tall, elderly pines occasionally shaded the trail. We could not see the West Fork, but we knew it was over to the west. A channel of stagnant water bound in rocky shores suggested that this canyon carried heavy water at other times of the year. The bed of the pond was covered in green scum, verdant with life living in the shallows.

Within half an hour we came to our first obstacle—a crossing of the West Fork. Since everyone was wearing leather hiking boots, we stopped and took them off to ford the river. This was a time-consuming task with a dubious reward of having to cross the stream barefooted. The cobble-stones were just small enough and covered in scum to present real problems for maintaining balance, but the cool water felt refreshing. The minute we exited a problem arose—with our feet covered in sand, we then had to put socks and boots back on. Now, on the west bank of the river, we climbed up among a scattered pine forest only to drop down to several river crossings in succession.

It was at this point that two important decisions were made by consensus. First, it was clear that it would take several years to walk the route if we kept removing our boots. Thus, we simply waded through the water in our boots—there were so many crossings that our boots and socks would remain perpetually wet. Boots offered better traction and protection from the rough stones than bare feet. Second, Bill, Claus, and Tim decided that a walking stick would provide balance in crossing the river. Tim began recording our crossings by cutting a notch in his staff.

At three miles we came to an Indian ruin across the West Fork. Up off the river about forty feet were the remains of what appeared to be a granary. One wall was still quite evident with tree posts used in building the structure in place. Off to the right was another depression, almost a cave, which had fallen into decay. Remnants had apparently slid down into the West Fork. Ancient people had trod these very paths, and we wondered whether they saw this wilderness as a comforting home.

Continuing through twisting canyons with walls rising steeply above us, tentlike rock formations came into view. The colors were mesmerizing, with red and ivory formations abounding. We were entering the fabled canyons of the Gila, where access out of the maze can be quite difficult, especially at points where the walls rise more than a thousand feet above the valley. Close inspection suggested avenues that provide a way out if needed, but then there was the problem of traversing the broad mesas.

Looking for a campsite in the dark canyon with a mild cooling wind, we found a suitable level site that had been used by others in the past. Bare ground and fire rings surrounded by logs are the common indicators of preferred campsites. Normally there are good reasons why others have camped in a specific spot before—level ground, availability of water and firewood, difficult terrain ahead that makes camping problematic.

There is a great amount of pleasure in finally realizing that you are at the end of the trail for the day. With an appealing campsite, your community begins to unfold. We set up our tents amid the brush and trees—enough privacy for each, yet closeness to build the bonds of friendship—and started a fire for cooking. This first night out was going to be extra special because our meal included filet mignon, baked potatoes, and salad. This was the last good meal we would see for a week.

Retiring early, I unfurled the elephant's foot and fluffed up the down coat. How would this high-tech combination work? An answer was forthcoming within an hour of settling into bed. I discovered that I was too hot, but that was comforting. Lying in bed, looking up through the mesh fabric of the little blue tent, I saw that the closeness of canyon walls and dense forest canopy obscured the stars despite almost total darkness and the crystal clarity of the air at six thousand feet.

Tent Rocks to Mountain Forest (Day Two)

The morning dawned fresh and bright, with a slight chill in the wind blowing down the canyon. Tim was first up and off to seek bird sightings. The rest of us assembled our packs after a quick breakfast. My staples for the next week would be hot chocolate, oatmeal, and breakfast bars. That sounds unappealing now, and it was unappealing then, but there was method to our madness. Our group was more interested in making miles than spending great effort on making breakfasts and lunches for which we were individually responsible. Dinner was a communal affair, with each person allotted two meals. Shared meals not only saved weight, but they also built camaraderie when replaying the events of the day—the highs and the lows along the trail.

After breakfast we headed up the West Fork, and at the first crossing Jim was able to navigate across a downed tree without getting his boots wet. He only delayed the inevitable. His bright red Kelty pack, with a faded yellow tent perched precariously atop it, swayed dangerously as he balanced on the beam. Bill followed gracefully without disaster. Claus and Tim just decided to get it over with and plowed through the water to the other side.

With twelve miles to go to White Creek, we cautiously walked, hopped, and jumped over and around rocks, tree limbs, and shrubs, exercising great caution owing to the urgent warnings of rangers. Rattlesnakes are prevalent in the Gila and must be given due respect. Consequently, much of the time our sight was focused on the ground looking for snakes, or at the rocky river bottom when crossing. Still, there were plenty of opportunities to appreciate the beauty of the Gila. In the narrow canyons pines tended to dominate with willows, box elders, locust, and cottonwoods along the water's edge. Fords across the river seldom saw water rising above our knees, but the water was clear and cold.

The West Fork murmurs along as a constant companion providing the central character of the canyon. High on the steep rocky walls, especially in the shade of the canyon, spruce and fir dominate the cliffs. In spots tent rocks assemble and add a riot of red color to the scene. The river bottom itself is mostly cobblestone, and fish fled when we splashed across the current, creating a bow-wave with our legs. Waiting on the other bank of every ford is a path of sand that soon balls up on boots and momentarily makes walking difficult. Meanwhile, the air temperature varies depending on the shade and vegetation. Not surprisingly, the farther up the canyon we went, and the higher the walls soared, the cooler it became.

One hour after breaking camp, we happened upon another campsite with its signature fire ring and logs. Glancing over to the fire pit, Claus noticed that smoke was rising almost imperceptibly in the air. We walked over to put the fire dead out and were shocked to discover that the previous campers had thoroughly doused their fire. Somehow, the fire had progressively smoldered underground and was heading toward dense brush. We rapidly dug out around the smoldering fire, only to find that the ground was extremely hot to touch. If it had reached dense vegetation there would have been a serious conflagration.

Pail after pail of water was poured on the fire resulting in billowing clouds of ash, steam, and smoke, but potential disaster was averted. We certainly did not blame the previous campers. They had poured plenty of water on the coals and ashes, but it just was not enough. This experience touched us deeply and we left committed to stirring all ashes and seeking hidden hotspots in the duff around fire rings.

By lunch we had arrived at Hells Hole—a canyon with magnificent walls and tent rocks. The West Fork lingers in this grotto with deep, clear pools that make fine swimming holes for the intrepid. It had been a pleasant walk to this point, however, the trail was seldom level. The ups and downs added together requiring a more strenuous effort than anticipated. Our full packs presented an additional challenge. Thus, at lunch we all were ready for a break. Nibbling away at our food supply, we jointly commented on the Gila as we found it versus the

Gila as we thought we would find it. Tim remarked on how disappointed he was in the bird life. He expected to see many more birds and much greater variety.

Beyond Hells Hole the trail wove through a wonderfully quiet forest of tall ponderosa pines. After wallowing through sand and river, the soft tread caressed our feet. A balsamy fragrance and rich scent of pitch swept over us as we continued to gain elevation. Now a little more than six hundred feet higher than when we first started, the forest and vegetation were changing significantly. Shrubs and deciduous trees were definitely not leafed out and the forest possessed that stark look so typical in winter. As we crossed the West Fork at Pine flat, the stream had diminished considerably since first stepping out on the trail. Formerly thirty feet wide at crossings, the river had narrowed to less than twenty feet across. The water was still crystalline clear with enticing pools, but its character was markedly different than down by the cliff dwellings. It was becoming a mountain stream rather than a canyon stream.

Jumping across the river to convenient rocks with the top-heavy pack swaying dangerously behind, I paused to look up at the sky. A clear turquoise had faded, and in its place was a white hazy overcast. There appeared to be no threat of rain, but the sun was obscured and the temperature was dropping without the intensity of sunny rays that had sought us out in the open stretches of the canyon. Even fewer bird sightings were occurring as we climbed up to White Creek Flat at seven thousand feet, our camp for the night.

On reaching the campsite our group went into action again. I went off in search of firewood and had to go a considerable distance to find even modest pieces of dry wood. Coming back with a meager load cupped in my arms, I looked up to see two tents already erect and a haggard-looking crew stretching their sore muscles. My first thought was, "What's wrong with this picture?" Jim had put on his trusty red vest. Tim was in a powder-blue down parka. Bill and Claus had on their dark mountain shell parkas. It then dawned on me that there was a discernible coolness in the air. What a difference a thousand feet can make in the mountains.

Jim, Claus, and Bill went off to fish, I set up my tent, and Tim chased birds. Above camp was a broad tranquil pond impounded by a beaver. The house made of weathered sticks was well sited near the eastern edge of the pond, but still far from shore and predators. Thirty- to forty-foot pines of modest girth flanked the West Fork. Tomorrow the trail would lead us up on Cub Mesa toward Turkeyfeather Pass, but for the moment we enjoyed the fruits of a long day and our mutual effort to negotiate the wilderness.

Trout that Jim, Bill, and Claus had caught supplemented dinner. Although you cannot deny how good trout taste after being pulled fresh from the stream, they do take a lot of effort to eat. These were not plump trout steaks that offered a lot of meat per bite. I spent more time picking bones out than seemed worthwhile—still hungry, I went looking for extra helpings of the macaroni and cheese. Given the meager breakfasts and lunches in my pack, I had a different expectation about dinner, envisioning a grand meal that filled you up—a woods person's meal. Instead, the portions were way too slim, and five hungry men were competing for extra servings. We went to bed hungry.

This combination of a modest dinner, gain in elevation, and the increasing cold of the high plateau and frigid air dropping down off 10,770-foot Mogollon Baldy Peak made for a very long night. I was hungry going to bed, and the situation was certainly not going to change during the night. Consequently, sleep eluded me because I was cold and uncomfortable. The skimpy sleeping bag and down coat were insufficient to keep me warm. While not in danger of becoming hypothermic, I was just uncomfortable enough to remain awake.

Sleepwalking with Friends (Day Three)

When morning arrived I felt completely exhausted, and the rush to down a meager breakfast did not help matters. Per camp custom, we boiled water and ate quickly in order to be on our way. I was dragging from the beginning, and my friends could tell that something was wrong. At one point or another along the trail that morning they would chat with me when walking or at a rest stop, offering their sympathies. I might be miserable, but at least I knew that others were looking out for me.

The trail climbed to eight thousand feet, coming out of White Creek flat under a cloudless sky, with the sun shining brightly as we progressed upward. The open forest had relatively little undergrowth among the oak, pine, and spruce. Several miles later, near Jackass Park, we came upon a mountain lion print on the dusty trail. Everyone was very excited about this discovery, but I was too tired to care and I just about dozed off as my friends examined the track. We hiked cautiously and quietly down Cub Creek hoping to see the feline, but we were not blessed with a sighting.

Turkeyfeather Pass is beautiful parkland of open meadow and spacious, towering ponderosa pine trees. Spruce and fir are spread throughout the taller ponderosas and rich green grass carpeted the ground beneath the pines. This is the Gila at its best. Judging by the limited undergrowth beneath the trees, this area does not receive much moisture. By now the day had mellowed and the pass provided the perfect opportunity to relax and enjoy the sun. It simply felt good to be warm again, and we sat in the sun soaking up its radiance. At 8,250 feet, the pass marked the high point of the trip.

The trail dropped down for another two miles toward Cooper Canyon where we found an idyllic camp among the spruce and confluence of Cooper Canyon and Iron Creek. An entire afternoon was still ahead of us so out came the fishing poles to catch diminutive and elusive trout in this creek. After fishing we stripped down for a bath in the icy waters of Iron Creek. It was cold but refreshing, and we romped like children until Jim brought out his camera and started taking pictures of the frolic. There were a lot of full moons on the rise.

Over a lingering dinner, Jim and Claus raised the issue about helping me catch up on sleep. Their concern was well received, although I stood there in a rather numb state, unable to enjoy the soft grandeur of the Gila. The group decided that I should sleep with Bill in his tent and Jim would switch to mine. They expected that I would sleep much better with increased warmth in the tent thanks to two people sharing the narrow confines. This was a gracious idea on my friends' part, but Bill snored up a storm, and although warm, I could not fall to sleep until well after midnight. But it was definitely much better being warm and sleepless than cold.

Cold Turkey(s) (Day Four)

The following day we headed east across a shoulder of the Jerky Mountains to the Middle Fork of the Gila River. We were all in a good mood, and the relatively level stroll offered fine views of the newly green oak-covered slopes of the Jerky Mountains and various canyons running east from their shoulders. Tim was in the lead ahead of me when he rounded a copse of trees and stopped to look back at us impatiently, wanting us to move faster. There ahead of him was a group of seven turkeys that he had not noticed. Pointing at Tim, I cried, "Turkeys, turkeys." Tim just thought I was kidding him, calling him a turkey. Fortunately, he turned around at the last minute as the turkeys soared over the edge of Clayton Mesa down into the forested valley below Clayton Spring. Tim was so excited. This was a bird he had been repeatedly trying to add to his life list. We all felt a deep sense of happiness for Tim and his achievement.

From the edge of Clayton Mesa we looked east to the distant Black Range and the Middle Fork, and then south to the Middle Fork's meandering course. Hillsides of the mesas and canyons were covered in oak and pine. Vegetation was sparse with lots of rough rock formations in this very rugged country. You could see the distinct change in microclimates between the higher pine- and fir-covered mesa and the lower oak and pine canyons. We would lose another six hundred feet to the Middle Fork, putting us a thousand feet lower in elevation than last night. Judging by the dry scene unfolding before us, I was certain that the cold nights would be left behind—deep sleep seemed a guarantee.

I took one last look to the ridges of the Jerky Mountains and Mogollon Baldy Mountain before dropping down to the Middle Fork. The high parks were just greening up and the new foliage was a shocking green. Below on the Middle Fork, huge cottonwoods were just beginning to leaf out. We zigzagged down the switchbacks and selected a campsite amid the lofty cottonwoods and green grass. Life suddenly opened up.

By the campsite I found a dead bald eagle. It was difficult to determine the cause of death, but we suspected that it had been shot. It must have been a magnificent bird in life, given its size. We continued across the Middle Fork drawn by a fantastic clump of claret cactus. Its deep red flowers served as a beacon, and bees were drawn in battalions to them. It gradually dawned on us that we were now in much warmer territory and might expect to see rattlesnakes. Our alertness went up a notch or two.

After dinner I retired to my tent under the cottonwoods. I loved this site because it was open and much warmer. I just knew that my troubles were behind me. Of course, that's when the slight, but persistent, breeze began to blow down the canyon. It seemed like the breeze just cut through the flimsy nylon tent. Sleeping by myself because we thought that the elevation was sufficiently low to ensure a warm night, I experienced a third night of sleep deprivation. In fact, it became so cold that I simply arose and started the campfire going, much to the distress of my companions. I kept a fire going all night long and was thankful for the lightening sky at dawn.

In the course of those early morning hours, freezing my tail off, I had plenty of time to think about this go-light ethic. My pack was superlight; I simply did not have sufficient clothing, bedding, or food for the Gila at this time of year.

These days the go-light fascination and fastpacking are the rage. Who can quibble with the thought of taking less rather than more so long as you do not suffer as a consequence? Mark Jenkins has argued in *Outside* magazine that no one purposefully wants to be a pack mule. Even from my initial days of hiking I always thought that the image of people trudging along with enormous weight on their backs was not the way to go. I cannot think of a backpack trip on which weight was minimal enough that I actually enjoyed the experience and at the same time was totally comfortable throughout the trip. Admittedly, my pack on this Gila trip was quite light, but for what good purpose?

Jenkins shares his religious conversion about taking less. Once he had been in a hurry to leave on a trip and had left out critical items—extra clothes. His partner had inadvertently left behind extra fuel, wind pants, and some food. They did without and learned that you can actually survive when you take less. Thus began a continuing challenge of lightening their packs. Each would cajole the other to leave something behind in a successive effort to reduce the stone they would be carrying on their backs.

This effort to pare down weight definitely has its advantages. You *can* make do with less. Once, on a hike in the Sangre de Cristo Mountains, I was several miles in when I realized that I left my tent poles back at home. This did not cause any major travail. I simply found dead-and-down vegetation to function as the supports. It was not elegant, and if a tremendous windstorm arrived, it would have been noisy. But the shelter would stand.

The point is to be prudent. For the Gila this would mean very light clothing for the day, but a down parka or vest for night and the early morning. This should save weight over a fleece jacket and long-sleeve shirt. In the San Juan Mountains of Colorado, you would increase the weight of your sleeping bag and add additional clothes, such as a light fleece jacket, that you would not take to the Gila. In both settings, precipitation is usually minimal except in thunderstorm season. In contrast, in the Pacific Northwest you would take more fleece items and fewer down items as the temperature range would be less dramatic.

I like to know with certainty that I can take whatever tough weather comes my way, be that in high desert, or the high country. I always carry more than needed, not to excess, for an extra margin of comfort. Most of my friends think I carry too much. However, if they spent three virtually sleepless nights in the Gila they would probably alter their habits as well. I do know this; in situations where I have had to put on all clothing in order to stay warm, I always have this slight sinking feeling about getting out of there safely. One thing is for certain: you never want the odds to catch up with you. That's when you never have to worry about how much you will ever carry again.

Friends to the Rescue (Day 5)

The following morning was a blur. We headed down the Middle Fork, and increasingly the canyon deepened. Trail and river meandered along, gradually losing elevation. Open, sparsely vegetated flats of Flying V Canyon and Swinging Cross Canyon were hot, dusty, and painful to cross. In my sleeplessness, I was having a tough time because the day's warmth made me want to stop for a nap. After more foot plodding, Clear Creek came into view and with it additional water volume that enlarged the Middle Fork. In my daze we came upon Trotter Cabin standing in an open meadow with sparse tall pines, cottonwoods, and junipers. Homesteaders must have been extremely hardy folk. My worries about sleeping at night would have made them laugh.

Trotter Cabin itself was returning to the earth. It had lost its roof and seemed to be stuck out in a fairly dry and unattractive setting. Rocky hills surrounding the cabin may have held the treasure that attracted this homestead, or this site was selected because it was the last large meadow before the canyon closed in. Over in the Middle Fork several blue herons gracefully stalked a pool for nourishment. There was wildness to the scene that tugged at your heart, even if you were too tired to enjoy it.

We finally reached a campsite deep in the canyon of the Middle Fork, and what a lovely scene it was. Tall ponderosa pines reached to the sky from the canyon's depth. They had a perfect climate of sun, shade, and water. The ground was covered in pine needles that added further to the ambiance. Down in the canyon, the harsh light of the upper Middle Fork was lost. Even in my drowsy state I felt blessed with the beauty of this wilderness canyon. Robust clumps of purple lupine blossomed victoriously in spots. Tentlike rock formations added colorful variety to the canyon depths. Shallow caves and intriguing depressions were everywhere. Things were looking up again.

After dinner my community of support came to the rescue. They informed me that I would sleep in the same tent with Claus in order to prevent me from being too cold. Bill loaned me an extra Pendleton shirt. Wow! What a night it was! I slept like the rocks that made up this canyon cathedral. In the morning Claus said, "You went to sleep the minute you put your head down. You started snoring right away and I was afraid to wake you seeing that you really needed the sleep." What a great sacrifice from a friend. At 6,500 feet, the night was much warmer than the previous night, even though we were sheltering in a canyon through which cold air was constantly flowing. Whatever the recipe, I slept the sleep of the dead. Morning was tremendous.

Encounter of the Fatal Kind (Day Six)

We continued to lose elevation as we approached an open area in the Middle Fork known as The Meadows. By now the canyon was enchanting, with the river twisting and turning constantly. Water levels had progressively risen as we dropped down the canyon. At twenty-five feet across, and with occasional deep pools, the river afforded us just plain fun. Here was the classic Gila. Walls towered above us for more than seven hundred feet. Tent rocks—pinnacles—provided a beauty that everyone could appreciate. A bright blue sky and blazing yellow sun were tempered by the constant interplay of shade in the bends. Tall pines provided coverage overhead. We continued to walk through refreshingly cool pools and crossings as the trail was often forced down into the middle of the canyon.

At one bend in the canyon, with the walls not more than forty feet across, the trail hung on a little lip of dirt over a deep pool of water. On the opposite rock face was a water ouzel nest, with the tiny gray young plainly visible. It would take a sharp eye by a predator to recognize the nest, for it looked like a rock. There above the deep pool the next generation was comfortably waiting for their afternoon meal.

Lunchtime was drawing near as we navigated the increasingly rocky trail. The rock spires towered overhead with copses of deciduous trees lining the river, having replaced the ponderosa pines. This portion of the canyon was routinely scoured by flash floods and high water that prevented the prospects of larger trees taking hold.

I opened my pack to find two lunches left, and neither amounted to very much. A small aluminum can of meat and crackers was about it for this lunch. I was so hungry after finishing this meager meal that I broke into a Snickers Bar as a way to fill up. Our only hope was that the fishermen would have better luck with trout. To this point the fishing efforts had produced dozens of the many suckers that scoured the stream's rocky bottom. Given their many bones and their penchant for bottom dwelling, we routinely threw these plentiful fish back.

The aluminum can crushed easily beneath my Vibram-soled boot. This was the sixth day out in the Gila Wilderness, and our remaining food was becoming not only sparse but also boring. Crackers that had begun the trip so fresh and neat in their plastic bags were now broken and crumbling due to the hot and dry conditions as well as having been loaded and reloaded within my pack. The chicken salad had tasted okay, but there just wasn't enough to satisfy that lingering hunger. I stuffed the trash bag back into my pack and tried to catch up with Bill. He was only fifty yards ahead of me, but he was moving fast, drawn by the progressive opening of the canyon. We were searching for The Meadows, which would be our camp for the night.

Bill turned around and paused for me to catch up. Ahead was the 113th river crossing of our trip. Every crossing had been notched onto his walking staff. By now it was just plunge ahead with rapid steps whenever the trail crossed the river. What a difference this was to the first tentative crossings where we carefully examined the riverbed, gauged the river's flow, and took precautions in the event of a slip.

Bill finished notching his walking staff as I bulldozed my way across the stream with a wake of rolling water pushed ahead by my passing. He took the lead and commented on the number of crossings and then looked back at my reaction just as he approached a gnarled white-gray cottonwood blocking the trail. He hesitated to lift his foot, and I almost walked into him. As he swung his foot over the log that terror of terrors sounded. Rattlesnake! The next few seconds passed in extreme slow motion as we tried to sort out the situation.

"Where is he? Where is he?" Bill cried. "It is over to your left. It is over to your left," I shouted. Bill was hung up on the log, having straddled it partially before coming to a stop. I tried to lift him and his pack back toward me. All we could hear was this loud sinister buzzing. Panic-stricken, his feet were flailing in the air, trying to get a purchase on anything that would get him away from the deadly rattle. After what seemed like hours, I finally pulled Bill back and we hastily retreated away from the log. Hearts were beating faster than we could believe. We were shaking—that was too close. Claus, Jim, and Tim came running up.

We retold the story over and over again with much laughter to ease the high anxiety. Then, we all walked over to take a look at the seven-foot-long monster as it slithered off toward the river. By the time the snake was well away from the log, we could see that it was more on the order of four feet rather than seven feet, but it was a thick specimen. The story was replayed once again from Bill's perspective and we all laughed. Then I said, "I'm glad that you took the lead after lunch, Bill. If it had been me with my longer stride, I would have walked right over the log onto the snake." The more I thought about it, the more I realized how close I had been to a potentially fatal encounter.

Tim notched yet another crossing while we stood silently, shifting our nervous feet, coming down from the event. Then, we slowly took off toward The Meadows. It was almost comical to see Tim and Claus in the lead with their walking staffs. They beat the grass and path furiously to detect snakes. After all these many days and nights in the Gila we had grown complacent about the prospect of running into a snake. Now we had encountered the reality that so many people have come to know in these canyons and mesas.

The grassy trail and opening canyon did indeed signal the beginnings of The Meadows. Perhaps a half-mile long and a bit less at its width, The Meadows lay six miles from the visitor center and our vehicle. It is a flat open area with very large, mature cottonwoods, box elders, oak, and pine, situated in the middle of the Middle Fork and thus a popular camping area. In addition to the trails coming from the north (down which we had traveled) and south by river, there is a trail from the West Fork over the mesa, and a trail out to the east.

I thought about other rattlesnake tales from the Gila. One of my friends had related his story about The Meadows. He and his partner were hiking out east above Indian Creek. They had just left The Meadows and were climbing up the trail that is rather steep in spots as it climbs almost eight hundred feet straight up. His friend was in the lead and reached up to a handhold on a rock. Unfortunately, a rattlesnake was already on that rock and bit the surprised hiker. Ron tells me that they discarded their packs and then ran to the truck. This was a matter of at least three miles. As Ron told the story, by the time they reached their truck, his partner's arm was swollen enormously. They drove to a ranger station that, as luck would have it, had a small plane. A pilot whisked the man to Silver City and medical attention. In the end it all came out okay, but Ron said he would never, ever go down to the Gila again.

Several years later we were camped down at The Meadows. As our group returned to the campfire and dinner after day hiking and fishing, a story was shared about another set of campers across the way. One of the campers owned a dog that had challenged a rattlesnake in The Meadows. The dog was bitten on the nose and was in excruciating pain. The poor owner had to borrow a handgun from some people on horseback. He shot his friend to put it out of its misery.

Having arrived at The Meadows just after lunch, we had most of the afternoon to fish, hang out, and explore. In many ways it was nice to be out of the dark canyon again and in a more spacious setting. The troops returned with enough fish to supplement the dinner because with only one more communal dinner left, the pickings were getting pretty slim.

Since we had dropped to almost six thousand feet, the day was extremely warm, and I guessed that night would be warm as well. It was, and I slept alone in my tent that night—or at least tried to sleep. We all were kept awake by a vociferous whippoorwill. A bright moon was out, and the bird just would not shut up. At first the calls were a novelty brimming with life and melody, but then they became a nuisance. It was acknowledging its territory and interest in establishing a family.

The Draw Toward Home (Day Seven)

The next day we climbed a thousand feet out of The Meadows to Woodland Park. The views to the north were beautiful with a clear, cool morning. We could see almost the entire way up to Snow Lake where we had begun the trip down the Middle Fork. Over to the east was a great view of Indian Creek and its tortuous, rocky, and winding canyon. Views to the south and the Middle Fork were all pine and fir on the mountainsides. As we looked west the expansive views of Mogollon Baldy and the West Fork drainage were well in view.

We walked along Woodland Park mesa to the south and came upon a great bald spot that heightened our ability to gain distant views. Walking was very mellow, with tread that was softened by needles from the junipers, piñon, and smaller ponderosa. The way dropped down several hundred feet into Big Bear Canyon. Here the ponderosa were more prevalent, thanks to an intermittent stream. A profusion of wild flowers, especially lupine, spread among the trees.

We hoisted our puny packs after a rest break; they had virtually nothing in them by this point. Climbing out of Big Bear Canyon, we came to a trail junction. One route led to the visitor center and the other to the West Fork. We took the latter. The trail became very rocky as we descended steeply into the canyon of the West Fork. The sharply vertical hillside was very hot with little shade from the low-growing trees. It was definitely dry and warm. White dust puffed up with each step.

At the bottom of the canyon we crossed the West Fork and joined the trail on which so many days earlier we had begun the trip. About two and a half miles from the trailhead, we sat down in the shade of some trees and crudely slaked our thirst. We had to go up the trail about a mile and a half to reach our first campsite. Sitting there sprawled out in the shade, our group had seen better days. Suddenly Jim suggested that it might be good to end our trip now rather than use another day in a site we had already enjoyed. Agreement was enthusiastic and unanimous.

There we sat for a few more minutes, a filthy bunch with scrapes on our legs and arms. Everyone's hair was greasy beyond belief. Collectively we were tired from the noisy whippoorwill night. The thought of cold drinks, hot showers, and substantial, tasty meals was overpowering. We were saturated with camping and quite honestly did not want another minute more. These are great moments to look back upon. You have had your fill of wildness and now want the best that civilization can offer. Home was all we could think about.

Looking back across the length of our trip in the Gila wilderness, I recognize the presence of community. Woven throughout the fabric of our wilderness experience was this fundamental reality—we looked after each other and shared, deeply, in many ways that are otherwise lost in city settings.

Seven

For a majority of the trip I suffered from a poor decision about equipment, especially the sleeping bag. My friends were very sensitive to this
dilemma and offered in a variety of ways to help me by providing various gifts, whether extra clothing, sharing a tent or a few well-timed
words of encouragement, or resting with me along the trail when they
wanted to be exploring or fishing. From our first step together, this
bunch of highly independent individuals relinquished personal agen-
das for my benefit.

Our Gila adventure is more than a tale of community focusing on
one person. It is about how the beauty, and challenges, of the wild
brings people together. Community was present in those last nostalgic
moments around a fading campfire, when the red-hot coals formed a
beacon in the night. The presence of the wild; the warmth of the coals;
the sights, sounds, and smells of the Gila; and the bonds of friendship
among those who know and love the earth drew us together around
that campfire.

Community was highly visible when Bill ran into the rattlesnake at
The Meadows. Our collective relief at his narrow escape was palpable.
The community had been threatened and successfully defended even
if luck was the preeminent player. Surely Bill heard from each of us as
we shared our concern and gratitude that he dodged this venomous
bullet. Then the forward guards protected the group by methodical vig-
ilance in searching for other rattlesnakes on or near the trail.

Our encounter with the flock of turkeys on Clayton Mesa reflects
additional insight on community. Tim had been drawn to this trip as
an instrumental way to add to his passion—his life list of birds. All of
us were feeling glum about the lack of birds in the Gila and Tim's sorrow
over the limited sightings. Thus, when we ran into the flock of
turkeys—a bird that Tim had been trying desperately to add to his life
list—there was considerable reason for all of us to share in his joy. The
spontaneity of the sighting added to our collective celebration.

In sum, wilderness trips, particularly multi-day adventures,
inevitably provide a ripe medium for the growth of communities. Not
too surprisingly, in wild areas people are drawn out of their cloistered
urban lives. There is cause to celebrate the bounty of nature, and there
are immediate, tangible reasons to band together for the common good.
This bonding creates community, and from it a culture that deeply loves
the earth.

Harmony
with
Nature

8
Technology Just Doesn't Matter

For many people, technology has been a primary determining factor that severs their harmony with nature. Lulled by a false sense of security in technological systems, contemporary society has broken its intimate connection with the earth. Wild lands and wilderness become something to dominate through technological means because we have deep faith in machines and human control over the environment. Of course, it only takes a massive flood, hurricane, excessive snow, drought, Arctic air mass, endless rains, or a September 11 to appreciate fully how pathetic technology is compared to the awesome power of nature and natural forces.

It is very difficult, if not impossible, to spend time in wild areas without realizing, or tuning into, the natural rhythms and relationships of our earth. As people leave behind their electronic toys, materialistic desires, infernal combustion engines, personal hatreds, squabbling, envy, and all other desensitizing and constraining factors that break their harmony with the natural world, the prospects for a culture that loves the earth multiplies.

Mountains, seashores and oceans, deserts, swamps, rivers, and prairies offer a tangible reminder of our connection with the earth. They are bigger than we, often towering over us, making us feel miniscule, and resisting our efforts at domination. Wildness encourages humans to remember the importance of balance with nature—a balance that has been lost in this age of technology and humanism. By letting go of our technological obsessions and systematically embracing wildness, opportunities build for a return to harmony between people and the land and an affirmation of the balance of nature and human endeavor.

"They were high above me on the ridge, lumping along like tortoises with deformed shells on their backs. Not only did they look uncomfortable, they certainly could not be having much fun." I shared these words with my parents after an enjoyable walk in the Angeles National

Forest. By day hiking, you can see much more than backpackers lumbering along under a tremendous load. What is the point of struggling along with all that weight? The point, as I would later find out, is the serenity and peace of spending a night away from civilization. The point is the ability to become immersed in nature relatively unfettered from the luxuries of a materialistic civilization. The point is to decouple for some hours and to savor the basics of life in a fundamentally profound way that leaves you in synch with nature.

It came to pass that I, too, was slowly drawn into the folly of walking with a forty-plus-pound pack on my back. But I did not go easily down this road, and my attempts to keep things in perspective often demonstrated an inability to learn from the wisdom of others. There were solid reasons why those packs are so heavy. There is essential gear that should be carried whether or not the person is a gearhead or equipment freak.

All who walk down a path with a pack on their back inevitably do one of two things. Either they stop backpacking because the load is too heavy and in the end kills the fun of doing it in the first place, or they begin to substitute lighter more technologically sophisticated equipment for the heavy stuff. And with these two alternatives, I too traveled the road of trying to lighten my load by more intelligent selection of gear. I spent almost an entire year planning for the new version of myself; a year spent mulling over catalogs and visiting mountaineering stores to determine what would work best to keep the weight down.

I was not at all eager to lug all that weight on my back. Thus began the slippery slope in spending lots of money to minimize the weight I carried. My attention focused on the basics—pack, tent, sleeping bag, and parkas. You can always get by on unappealing food, but you have to keep yourself protected from the elements. I owned a Kelty frame pack with a padded belt, weighing four and a half pounds. Internal frame packs had been on the market for years, but I did not like how they ride on the back. The beauty of the external frame is the ability to keep the pack off your back and hence keep you cooler. Contemporary external frame packs have fancier belts to improve comfort, but they tend to be heavier and awkward.

The tent was a different matter. I still owned a classic A-frame tent that was voluminous and had seen many miles. However, this tent was well beyond seven-plus pounds and bulky. I wanted something that weighed half this amount. Early Winters had introduced a Gore-Tex tent that was very light—around three and a half pounds. It was single-wall construction with a big hoop at the front and a smaller hoop at the rear.

The sleeping bag was a no-brainer. I owned a Holubar bag rated to fifteen degrees. The bag was made up in Colorado and had received favorable reviews in the backpacking/mountaineering community. With 60 percent of its down fill on top, the bag was very slim and weighed in at two and a half pounds. That seemed like a perfect weight. Pack, sleeping bag, and tent weighed about ten pounds—a good benchmark for the foundations.

Now for the parka and insulation. Patagonia had just introduced a new parka that wore like iron and was completely waterproof. This was my choice, having seen too many Gore-Tex parkas fail in the field. In terms of insulation, a full down parka was too much protection and weight. Synthetic parkas were too heavy. I selected a high-quality down vest that functioned like a toaster oven. The other assorted gear and food were added to these fundamentals. My pack was definitely in the high twenty-pound range, meaning it was heavy by today's standards for "fastpacking." Nonetheless, it was durable and adapted to the serious mountain terrain encountered in the San Juan and Sangre de Cristo Mountains, where elevations ranged from ten thousand to thirteen thousand feet.

In late July, we decided to visit the Weminuche Wilderness. The plan was to head up Hope Creek, with its initial elevation of 9,700 feet, and climb to the Continental Divide at 12,000 feet. Mount Hope was the centerpiece, looming at 12,800 feet. On a warm and beautiful summer day, we drove over Wolf Creek Pass to the trail. Water was everywhere, running down the mountainsides and creating little lakes and tarns at the pass. The entire divide was glorious in greenery except for the numerous and most stubborn snow patches. Wildflowers were just hitting their stride. This was summer at its finest. As we crested the pass before noon, only a few clouds marred an otherwise perfectly clear azure sky.

We met our friend Dick, who had driven down from Colorado Springs, in the parking lot at Big Meadows Reservoir. Bill and Don had ridden up from Albuquerque with me. It was comforting to be back in the company of friends, ready to hit the trail. After exchanging greetings and eating lunch, we began to load up. Don was famous for carrying the oldest, most despicable-looking gear on these trips. But he never seemed to suffer. He was a great person to go with because he had few complaints and "just did it." There is no finer fly fisherman than Don, but he carried the most depressing-looking vest and rod. The Isaac Walton League would have him arrested. Nonetheless, the real test came when the line went in the water. All the way up the trail, whenever he saw someone with a rod coming the other way, he would ask about the fishing. To a person they replied that the fish were just not biting. Within the afternoon he would prove these erstwhile fishermen wrong as he caught several keepers for dinner.

We started on the relatively level trail climbing along the north side of Hope Mountain and across Hope Creek. The dense spruce, fir, and aspen forest had seen recent rain and the tread of the trail was very damp. Within ten minutes we stopped to adjust packs—everyone except Don and myself. Our packs were sufficiently light that walking was not the chore that the others complained about. I smiled smugly. All of my planning was paying off. Hope Creek tumbled nosily to our left, where it was constantly dropping a foot here and a foot there. It swirled around bends. Most of all, Hope Creek was crystal-clear. Sun sparkled off the clear gravel and rocks in the streambed. Little cascades and waterfalls formed wherever logs had the audacity to block its progress.

Twenty minutes up the trail we entered a large open meadow, the work of beavers. A marsh below the trail was with thick, rich grasses standing tall in the quiet water. A cloud passed overhead chilling the moment. Don looked valiantly for fish. "Come on, Don," we scolded, "There will be plenty of fish further up." It was all we could do to keep him focused. At the upper end of the meadow, a group of trees formed a fine camp. A bit buggy due to the meadow, it was just not far enough in for us, having driven this great distance—a perfect camp at some other time.

The next two miles the trail climbed steadily up to our camp at 10,600 feet. The way was punctuated by a progression of avalanche slopes. We would hike for ten or fifteen minutes in the forest and then come out onto these brushy slopes. The forest was monochromatic, with evergreens dominating the landscape and limited undergrowth. Each successive stand of trees was smaller than the previous grove; thus, we could mark our passage upward by their height. The trail tread was fairly soft, with occasional dirt and rocks where trail erosion had occurred. Then, suddenly, we would reach a clearing demarcating an avalanche path, and the tread would become hard and rocky, with lots of running water. A profusion of subalpine shrubs and bushes shouldered the trail on each side. Amid this setting, cow parsnip, yarrow, columbine, and other mountain flowers grew aggressively. I could almost feel the growth that was occurring at this time of year. Summer was short and these plants were making the most of the sun, water, and soil.

Avalanche chutes were dimpled with the usual evidence of powerful snow slides. Trees were broken off about six feet above the ground. Occasionally we would come upon a set of new casualties: very large white bark pine that had been felled the previous winter. Trees that reached almost a century of life were snapped to pieces in seconds. This was an awesome, inspiring thought. The rich, sweet smell of pine wafted through these clearings as the warm sun heated the resins—a parting gift from the dead. Avalanche chutes also helped us to measure our progress up the side of Mount Hope. Clearings offered visual confirmation of our progress toward the Continental Divide.

At three miles we reached a campsite sheltered in numerous pines. This was a good location because it was low enough to avoid lightning on the divide, but high enough that the trail went straight up from this point on its final push to the crest. Hope Creek splashed joyously to our immediate south about fifty yards away. The divide loomed above us to the west. Out to the east we could see the ramparts of the divide and to the east the South San Juan Wilderness. To the north was mountainside. After making camp, Don was off in a flash to catch fish after erecting the most pathetic-looking dome tent. Dick, Bill, and I decided to hike up the mountain a ways. Two hours later we were enjoying a campfire and dinner.

The night passed uneventfully and the morning dawned crisp and clear. Following a communal breakfast, Don again went off to slaughter the fish. He had caught two small fish the day before. One that he kept and ate for dinner was a legal catch, while the other went back for fattening up. Don just loved to catch and eat fish. He was a catch-and-release fisherman when he had what he wanted for dinner, or when the fish was below the size limit. The rest of us headed up the trail.

This last portion to the divide was a good climb. Half of the way was through dense forest and the rest was meadow with stands of trees. The switchbacks ground upward. In a clearing we came upon a hunters' blind made of plywood and branches weathered to a fine patina. This clearing was approximately one hundred yards long and fifty yards wide. It was essentially a mass of skunk cabbage. There are not supposed to be any structures in the wilderness, but this one had escaped the Forest Service and somehow seemed a part of the mountain.

Technology Just Doesn't Matter

Our trail turned east and climbed in several switchbacks above the clearing where the upper ramparts of the divide were visible. There was a difference in the air—simultaneously hot and cold with a distinct dampness. Clouds continued to build and to obscure the sky. Normally in thunderstorm season the storms do not really build until mid-afternoon, but we could tell that things were progressing much faster than normal and it went unspoken among us—a thunderstorm was going to threaten sooner rather than later on this day.

We neared the final five hundred feet of elevation gain, passing a camp along the way. This was dangerous territory with scattered white bark pine spread haphazardly. Larger specimens bore witness to the electric conflagrations of the summer storms. A small group was camped around the trees. They had a pretty little stream outside their door but the extremes of weather and altitude were apparent. The inhabitants had on twice as much clothing as we. They looked like they were in siege warfare against the weather and mountain. This drab and dismal portrait reminded me of how high we were on the divide. We continued two hundred feet to tree line and spacious meadows with wildflowers everywhere. The scale of this basin just below the Continental Divide was hard to perceive. Everything looked so close, yet when you saw a distant herd of mule deer climbing above the basin you began to realize just how enormous everything was in proportion.

By now the clouds were building in an ugly way—fat, dark, ominous, and noisy. Thunder occasionally broke the air. Breezes became wind. Warm became cold. You knew what was coming next. Not wanting to serve as a lightning rod, we started down the trail. Just above the high camp we reached a nice spot to stop for lunch. I no sooner had cheese and sausage on my egg bagel than the first squall hit. Hail came raining down out of nowhere despite the fact that the clouds were not particularly massive above us. In fact, it was quite clear to the east. We scurried to throw on raingear and to hustle down the trail. But in five minutes it was all over, and we were dropping below the high camp. I marched along with a smug confidence in my new raingear. It was tough, almost brittle, and not very comfortable, but this was what it was all about—harsh conditions and life-threatening possibilities if our gear failed.

The rest of the way back to camp passed quickly. As with so many other times in these situations, I merely needed to go through the effort of putting on all my raingear to stop the precipitation. We peeled off our gear and wound down the mountain against a background of grumbling from overhead. It was difficult to see any lightning, but the constant thunder implied a gloomy day on the divide. I could not help but think of those in the high camp who were prisoners of their tent. Why not hike down to a lower elevation where the day would be better spent? High country ramblings were already done for the day. At least they could enjoy the beauty of a forest camp rather than the monotony of a ripstop nylon wall.

Later in the afternoon as we lingered around the camp, the storm reached a second peak. In a flurry of huge raindrops we rushed for cover under the trees. Then, seconds later, we dove for our tents as a full-fledged hailstorm raked our camp. Bill and I fought to get inside the new tent. "Hey," Bill cried, "It's cold out there." Yes, it was cold. We climbed into our bags for warmth. I donned my thermal underwear top and down vest. Hail continued to tear at the tent. "Nothing like a real test," I said to Bill as my eyes wandered around the tent to see whether it would stand up to this onslaught. Suddenly a single-wall tent didn't seem like such a great idea. Sure, I had saved weight, but if the worst hail broke through our single membrane, we were in major trouble. The safety of a fly seemed so apparent now. Images of slightly heavier, more solid fly and tent combinations that I eschewed raced through my mind. And then the hail really increased. It accumulated rapidly on the ridge of the tent, and we pounded off the growing mounds to prevent the tent from collapsing.

The racket was unnerving while thunder boomed. There is nothing quite like being in the middle of such a storm just off the Continental Divide. Rain and hail pelted the tent so I snuggled deeper in my gear and found that it was getting very cold. If this kept up it was entirely feasible that I did not have enough insulation for the conditions. Just as these thoughts crossed my mind, good old Bill pointed it out: "There's water leaking in at our front." The storm was pounding on our front door, and now there was water leaking in through the seams along a zipper. So much for the beauty of a Gore-Tex tent. This was bad. And then, just as disaster seemed imminent, it stopped.

We left the tent and surveyed the damage. Hailstones were strewn everywhere. The temperature must have dropped at least twenty degrees to the high thirties. In the interests of saving a few pounds, I had broken one of the rules of safe camping. My "go-light," "fastpacking" gear was not suitable for the conditions or my body's needs. Only with the sudden appearance of the sun did I calm down. I could not believe how suddenly things had changed. I could not believe that even in my sleeping bag with all my clothes on I had suddenly became quite chilled. I resolved in my mind to take care of this matter the moment I reached home.

I had sadly placed my faith in technology as a means to enjoy the wilderness. In many respects I challenged nature with an in-your-face attitude that light equipment will stand up to the rigors of high-altitude camping. In fact, the equipment was incorrect for the setting. I was out of harmony with the very mountains that I came to enjoy. Equipment failure meant that my communion with nature was depreciated. It is tough to think lofty thoughts about the earth and wildness when you are freezing.

And where was Don? He turned up about an hour later looking like the cat had just dragged him back to camp. For the very first time in years of camping together he came to me and asked for extra clothing—of which I had precious little. "What happened," I asked. "Did the storm get you?" Don replied, "It wasn't the storm that did me in. That was no problem. I just holed up under a tree and waited it out. Had a bite to eat. I had found a good fishing hole and I wanted to finish it. I hardly got wet. However, when I crossed the creek I slipped and fell in. I'm freezing. It was a long, long walk these last thirty minutes." We swaddled Don in warm clothing and he retraced his fishing success. He brought back one lunker and two medium-size rainbows. He was a happy, but cold man. Fifteen minutes later he was warm and preparing the fish for the evening's meal.

Returning home, I reflected on my disappointment with the trip—how survival became the overriding concern instead of enjoying the bounty of the mountains. Out of harmony and maintaining an obsessive belief in equipment, I was less able to hear the song sung by the rollicking Hope Creek; to enjoy the frosty morning after a brittle cold summer night; to share talk with close friends about the bigger issues of life; or to appreciate the beauty of aspen trees with their fragile leaves blowing in a down-canyon breeze.

I went on a shopping spree to shore up my inadequate equipment. There is nothing macho about being cold and miserable in the mountains. The first order of business was a new tent. The local mountaineering store carried a three-hoop style, five-and-a-half-pound, North Face tent that could stand up to anything. The rain fly covered the entire tent except the front door, which was coated nylon. There was no vestibule. Sadly, some years later, North Face "improved" the tent by adding a weighty vestibule that raised the tent's weight to over six and a half pounds.

Next I purchased a Sierra Designs sleeping bag rated to minus five degrees. That was warm. I already owned an ancient hooded down parka by Sierra Designs that I used for snowshoeing. This would henceforth replace the down vest. I was all set, and this combination immediately proved highly successful on a low twenty-degree morning at Vallecito Creek in Colorado. As I lay in the tent with the door open, the previous night's condensation froze while I lay there toasty warm. A fifteen-degree bag for the high country—no way. Of course, there are situations where light is right. You just need to be careful to select the right equipment for the right situation and build in for a margin of error.

As the years slip by and equipment shows its age, there is an inevitable struggle to replace certain pieces. This should be no problem as the technology of mountaineering/backpacking equipment continues to progress each generation, with iterations of small improvements. But has the technology of outdoor equipment really improved? Research and development has produced better materials in strength and reduced weight. More sophisticated designs have evolved with a proliferation of manufacturers. Sure, the small proprietary operations are pretty much gone, swallowed up by larger corporations. Nonetheless, there is clearly much more choice as far as equipment is concerned. Or is there?

With few exceptions, equipment today is fundamentally heavier and needlessly more complex than twenty years ago. It is certainly more expensive. It may be marginally more functional. I think that these trends point to a continuing revolution in gear. Let's revisit the ancient gear that hiking elders used to better understand the roots of the looming paradigm shift in outdoor equipment. The best place to start is the single most important piece of gear—the parka. Without a parka to repel rain or to block wind, hikers are exposed to the vagaries of weather. Granted, a wool (or these days, synthetic) cap offers the best way to keep warm for a minimum amount of weight, but without a shell to repel the elements, a wool cap cannot be completely functional.

More than twenty years ago I purchased a blue coated-nylon parka from Recreational Equipment. I still have it and use it when painting around the house. This parka is extremely lightweight. It has three medium-sized cargo pockets in front; elastic cuffs with snaps; a drawstring hood; a drawstring at the waist to keep out wind and snow; and absolutely no lining. This parka has stopped gale force winds at

Berkeley Park on Mount Rainier and at Red Pass in the Glacier Peak Wilderness. I have never, absolutely never, been wet when wearing this parka. On trips where there has been day after day of rain and snow, the parka worked. Was condensation a problem? Not really; I simply wore a T-shirt under the parka.

After too many trips I began to suspect the integrity of the coating and switched to a piece of armor manufactured by Patagonia—a completely water-resistant shell. Unlike the coated parka, this impenetrable barrier was stiff and a little too uncomfortable. I then switched to a Gore-Tex parka by North Face. That parka is heavier, less flexible, less comfortable, and five times more expensive, but impervious to moisture. Today, the choice in high-tech parkas is almost limitless, but have we really made progress?

The typical contemporary backcountry parka is made from a Gore-Tex laminate or derivative. It has zippers under the armpits and zippered pockets, as well as zippered vents on the front, side, and back. It is lined with mesh to help transfer water vapor. Unlike my original rain parka, the contemporary model has a storm flap over the front zipper, which is secured with Velcro and/or snaps. The cuffs generally incorporate Velcro or elastic. The typical parka costs at least five times what my simple parka did two and a half decades ago, and it weighs a pound and a half—that is, almost twice what my original parka weighs. Am I better off with this new parka? The answer is yes if we can imagine some extreme conditions that the vast majority of us will never encounter. The answer is no considering the conditions even radical hikers and backpackers face. Most contemporary parkas are excessively complex, heavy, and expensive. And, when it comes time to load this parka in a pack, it will provide an illusion of safety while adding weight to the pack beyond all reason.

Outdoor equipment manufacturers have greatly differentiated their product lines, for example, offering dozens of parkas for a wide variety of specific activities. Are we better off because of this greater variety? In many respects, climbers, hikers, backpackers, skiers, and runners are superficially at less risk due to the wider variety of equipment tailored to specific situations. There is a parka for every condition. Equipment suppliers have segmented natural environmental conditions to establish niches within niches. A parka is not designed just for climbing, but for bouldering in desert canyons or for challenging extreme big wall conditions.

Segmentation of the natural environment ensures that consumers must acquire the right piece of gear for the right conditions. Since so many of us must live our passion vicariously through the myth and romance of equipment catalogues and outdoor magazines, the purchase or conspicuous consumption of gear allows us to feel satiated, as though we have participated when in reality the experience was only visual and virtual. We have the gear, therefore we climb, hike kayak, bike, and so forth—if only in our minds.

Yet, even as the absurdity of equipment segmentations unfolds a counterrevolution in mountaineering, hiking and outdoor equipment is proliferating. In part this revolution is generated by an ascetic philosophy that people embrace when they are involved in outdoor activities. A disgusted class of consumers who are sick of materialism and oversaturation by corporate advertising provides further fuel to forces of change. Baby boomers, post-baby boomers, and Generation X, Y, and Z consumers are seeking equipment alternatives that allow them to function at very high levels, as they did in their youth. They are more interested in achieving balance with nature. This revolution is not motivated by technological innovations in materials or fashion developments, but by the desire to have the most functional, lightest-weight, best-value-priced gear. To understand what this revolution implies, consider the contemporary parka or tent.

Most mountain parkas see the vast majority of their action on urban and suburban streets, malls, and soccer fields. They look great, send an impressive message, and perform beneficial functions. However, most mountain parkas are way too heavy for their intended use. They typically weigh two pounds plus owing to unnecessary bells and whistles.

The profile is generosity—generosity with functions that arguably add limited functional value, but that add enormous weight and cost. Certainly these parkas convey an image of invincibility and vigor as well as affluence. Do consumers really want the superfluous gewgaws? The industry has been dictating products that are antithetical to the experience. We do not want more conspicuous consumption and useless technology. We want high-quality and low-cost equipment with great function, low weight, and impressive style. Under these conditions we are more prone to a harmonious relationship with the environment.

"Serious" backpacking tents available for two people have been tarted up to the point that they weigh more than eight pounds. For the solitary hiker who does not want to be jammed into a sardine can for the night, this is excessive weight. My North Face mountain tent purchased fifteen years ago was designed for winter conditions—the kind of conditions that you can easily face at high elevations any time of the year. This 5.5-pound tent was a model of simplicity and function. The tent poles were lightweight and thin aluminum—not the massive poles available today. The tent was very parsimonious in the use of fabric for the body. A three-hoop design minimized the amount of fabric required, and its high center pole provided height and space. Because there was no vestibule, I could exit and enter the tent with ease. The streamlined design meant that I never had to guy out the fly despite hurricane winds. Best of all, I did not begrudge carrying the weight. There were no mesh panels to allow excessively cold air or wind to disturb sleep. In short, this tent displayed the proper balance of form, function, economy, and quality.

How laughable to compare this gem with an "updated" tent purchased last year. This tent weighs about seven and a half pounds, almost eight when you include the stuff bag and stakes. It has three poles like my former tent, but they are about twice the weight because they are twice the length. The tent has two doors and two vestibules and a zippered panel for a skylight. With two doors, why would you need this panel? For ventilation? Of course, the panel does not work when the fly is overhead. This model tent has more zippers than you can imagine—which spells weight.

What's amazing is the lack of progress in the space of fifteen years. We have the most advanced fabrics and computer-aided design and manufacturing processes ever available. Yet the result is a tent that leaks like a sieve and whose fly fails to keep out water. Who is designing these monstrosities? Do they ever go out and use their products in the field? Or do they just sit around and play with their computers? It certainly makes you wonder, doesn't it?

Not every equipment manufacturer or retailer has followed this herd mentality to expensive, heavy, nonfunctioning equipment. One such firm is GoLite, established in 1998 by Kim and Demetri Coupounas. GoLite's struggle to survive was chronicled in the December 1999 issue of *Outside* magazine. GoLite's mission is to "design, manufacture and sell the best ultra-lightweight . . . equipment in the world." Thus they have targeted a niche that the big boys have ignored—function and simplicity over fashion. GoLite manifests an attitude of innovation in an industry that is not driven to excel.

Eight

Is this another David and Goliath story? From all appearances this is precisely what GoLite faces. GoLite projects spending at least a million dollars just to launch its line of ultra-lightweight equipment, and allocating almost another half-million dollars just to complete a second production run. Does this business stand a chance?

GoLite's strategy is based on the "Ray-Way," a philosophy of backpacking articulated by Ray Jardine in *Beyond Backpacking* and the *Pacific Crest Trail Hiker's Handbook*. The essential Ray-Way is to drive down the weight of your pack so that you can hike vast distances. Lighter weight means an ability to cover more ground, which means you need to carry less. He advocates an eight- to ten-pound total pack weight for all your needs except food. Needless to say, this sort of metric requires the very lightest gear.

Jardine is not just a vocal prophet. He has proven his method walking the Pacific Crest Trail and the Appalachian Trail. He admits that his approach is not designed for everybody. You must keep moving to stay warm. You must consume wholesome foods. You must wear light athletic shoes to save weight. You must. . . . Well, you get the picture. Deviate from the regimen and you are doomed. The Ray-Way is a total approach to hiking long distances fast. Once a hiker has reached the day's multi-mileage destination, then it's into a down quilt for the night before starting the race all over again.

Demetri Coupounas was inspired by Jardine's system as a method to reduce the base weight of a backpack load. To achieve this goal it is necessary to reinvent backpacking gear. This is easier than it sounds. Fanatical attention must be focused on cutting out all superfluous features within equipment. GoLite has attempted to adopt a conservative interpretation of the Ray-Way. This may be going a little farther than necessary, especially when considering market potential.

A relatively small percentage of hikers, most of them young, are physically able to stand up to the rigors of the GoLite approach. Thus, the market for these goods is very limited compared to the larger market of backpackers who do not hike very long distances, yet could use a break from the maniacal weight added to their gear by the equipment purveyors. The Ray-Way and GoLite are not panaceas, but a good idea that the large retailers and manufacturers should consider.

The beauty of the GoLite approach is its commitment to efficiency and function. Their parka is minimalist—no bells and whistles. The parka shell is not waterproof—you use a small umbrella to keep rain off when hiking. However, it is windproof and useful for repelling mosquitoes. The parka has three zippers to support two pockets and the main zipper of the body. It weighs two-thirds of a comparable waterproof parka and costs about one-half compared to its competitors. The parka and the backpack are the high points of the GoLite line.

GoLite is not selling just any piece of equipment. It is selling a philosophy, a system, for backpacking. This is certainly a good idea. However, large manufacturers are emulating the best of GoLite's approach; that is, cutting out all the unnecessary gewgaws and driving equipment back to a sane level. The larger production runs of the big manufacturers will help to substantially lower costs. This may mean the end of GoLite. GoLite's best hope is to cross over into other outdoor recreation areas besides backpacking.

The minimalist approach is cautiously surfacing among the dominant manufacturers. It is most apparent in rain and wind parkas that incorporate only the essentials. For most large manufacturers, this may just be a loss leader to protect their market domination. With luck, the field is looking for ways in which to design products that function first and cater to fashion second. But that seems unlikely.

The materialist mentality ingrained within our culture is that more is better. Overdesign ensures that our equipment will enable us to survive in the Arctic, even if the mass of us will never set foot there. Still, the thought of cutting my load, whether day hike or backpack, in half is a romantic notion I cannot relinquish. I dream dreams of the manufacturers taking advantage of all the advanced materials and computer-aided design to build a tent for two people that offers some height (that is, greater than forty inches in the interior) with proper ventilation, the ability to withstand any weather—rain, humidity, snow, hail, or sun—without crumbling, and a weight of four pounds. Or producing a minimalist shell that can fend off rain or snow and cold while weighing in at less than one pound.

Until equipment manufacturers shift their paradigm of thinking away from mass-market fashion and to the task at hand, we are doomed to see more of the same in outdoors equipment. Perhaps young recreationists will rebel by demanding a dramatic change in the industry. In the long run, it just does not matter. As my friend Don has shown time and time again, it is not the gear that makes the outdoors person. It is the simple act of getting out there and making do with what you have brought along. There is no one best way to hike, camp, backpack, run, ski, snowboard, bicycle, or roller blade. There is only the doing of it.

High-technology mountain gear—fuchsia packs, day-glo orange parkas, permeable/impermeable membrane rain pants, zero micron water filters, supersticky climbing shoes, and all of the other paraphernalia—is a wonderful thing to behold. However, equipment is only the means to an end, and that end is developing a closer relationship with the earth. High-tech gear can provide some assistance in enjoying nature, but its contribution is really only marginal at best. In many respects, obsession with equipment only denigrates our interaction with nature and thus disrupts the harmony that we are seeking to achieve.

There is an almost fatal attraction to the outdoors equipment advertised in glossy sporting magazines such as *Outside*, *Backpacking*, *Audubon*, and *National Geographic Adventure*. Healthy young people with smiling faces and the latest technology are portrayed in the most exotic locations, having enormous fun, and conquering legendary peaks, rivers, or calamitous conditions. The ads never are able to show the high humidity, stench of fear, incessant black flies, intestinal parasites, or other adverse conditions often associated in just reaching these locations.

Technology perpetuates a myth that we will, as the Eddie Bauer advertisements suggest, actually "Take the day off. Call in well." Or, as a Sierra Designs ads suggested, forgo that baby shower in order to enjoy an afternoon of hot cross-country skiing. The advertisements convey an image that we want of ourselves—healthy, vibrant, courageous, forever young, physically fit, and sexually attractive. And there's the rub. We want to buy an image rather than wildness.

Technology inevitably severs our intimate relationship with nature and in the end disrupts our harmony with the earth. No set of ultimate gear guarantees that we will focus on what is most important. Successive efforts to refine the equipment we use as an instrument to enjoy wildness—such as obsessive attention to reducing weight of backpacking gear—typically lead to further imbalance. Nature expects much more from us, and that is our full attention, not just a passing glance at a beautiful scene or good thoughts about having encountered a charismatic animal. Only by concentrating on our balance with nature will we ever build a culture that deeply loves the earth.

9

Rambling along Rainforest Paths

Our society repeatedly attempts to control nature in large-scale ways under the guise of protecting the common good. John McPhee examined the futility of this presumptuous thinking in *The Control of Nature*. Whether through the U.S. Army Corps of Engineers' efforts to tame the Mississippi River, Iceland's struggle to halt the flow of red-hot molten lava from overwhelming the island of Heimaey, or Los Angeles's system of dams designed to halt calamitous floods from the San Gabriel Mountains, humans cling to the optimistic notion that they can in some fashion control vast natural forces.

Edward Abbey often raised a spirited voice against silly attempts to dam the Colorado River, the disquieting result of Lake Powell and attendant urban sprawl in Phoenix and other cities of the Southwest supporting the dam in the first place. Abbey argued persuasively that Lake Powell is merely a very large holding pond designed to trap sediment and to serve as an enormous evaporation pool for the misspent Colorado River. Since the reservoir will ultimately backfill with sediment, it is only appropriate to remove the dam now and let nature resume its course.

A similar folly involving water, but on a much smaller scale, surfaces in Pete Fromm's *Indian Creek Chronicles*. The Idaho Department of Fish and Game created an eighty-yard-long, six-foot-wide salmon channel on Indian Creek, which empties into the Selway River in the Selway-Bitterroot Wilderness. The idea was meritorious—reintroduce salmon by bringing in eggs from Idaho hatcheries each fall and allowing the eggs to settle in the channel. With a clean gravel bed and plenty of fresh water, the salmon would hatch and repopulate the river and nearby streams.

Unfortunately, this endeavor requires a constant flow of fresh water—a significant difficulty in winter, when the Selway-Bitterroot Wilderness experiences frigid Arctic temperatures. Thus, Pete Fromm was assigned to keep the channel bottom clear of ice by chopping away any buildup at the drop-off, a task requiring fifteen minutes each day. Fromm's book replays the interminable hours of loneliness and isolation in the wilderness as well as the heroic struggle against body-sapping cold. Having controlled nature and killed off the salmon, another technological fix is used to right a wrong. Yet that technology was not greatly harmonious in the natural scheme of things. Of the more than two million eggs Fromm nurtured, fewer than twenty fish returned four years later.

Ogallala Chief Luther Standing Bear suggested that only white men see the land as wilderness, something that must be brought under domination. We perceive that nature threatens us and therefore must be subjugated for our safety and progress. The Native American tradition, in contrast, does not characterize wild lands as threatening. In fact, wilderness is seen as just the opposite by Native American cultures— abiding beauty and serenity.

Our approaches to wilderness travel these days are very symbolic of the control ethos. For many, wilderness presents danger and physical challenges to overcome. Proper high-tech equipment must be assembled in order to ensure safe and comfortable passage. Only secondarily does our thinking reflect the beauty that might unfold in a long trek through wild lands—a mountain meadow filled with purple-blue iris, stands of white lupine, and red Indian paint brush in the shady margins; a crystal-clear flowing stream over a sunlit cobblestone bottom that makes your soul leap with excitement; soft red-yellow-gold alpenglow on sawtooth peaks above a glacial lake. We are programmed to think first of the challenge and second of the beauty because wilderness is a threat.

A culture that loves the earth looks beyond efforts to control nature and upholds the idea that wildness is essential for progression of civilization. Unfettered by frivolous concerns about dominating wilderness, opportunities unfold to appreciate and enthusiastically treasure our walk on this magnificent earth.

Having started up the trail only five minutes earlier, I was already removing my boots to cross the ten-foot-wide stream slipping purposefully through the dense alders. We looked left and right, but no rocks protruded above the swift current and rapidly flowing milky-white stream. This opaque coloring was not the result of glacial melt, although the Quinault River starts as a trickle in the snowfields of the Olympic Mountains. Rather, clay-like banks of this slough helped to give body and definition to the flowing stream. Here, in early June, mountains of the Pacific Northwest were still giving up the bounty from a normal winter—essentially seven months of clouds, rain, and snow. Some weeks later, this channel of the Quinault would be dry as a bone and others following would only note a boggy area that dipped in the gentle rise and fall of trail toward the heart of the wilderness on the Olympic Peninsula.

Jim was first to remove his boots, and he plunged into the middle of the river—the essence of the Olympic National Park. "Yikes! That's cold! Whoee." Just what I needed to hear. I finished pulling my boots off. They were still pristine with their shiny coat of grease designed to repel water. I carried a small tin of additional grease to apply at the end of each day. Wet boots can become a very depressing fact of life out on the trail.

I shivered in the slight breeze, holding boots in hand, ready to die my little death. Would this become a constant challenge on the trail? We had not anticipated a river crossing so immediately on this almost fifty-mile walk through the heart of a wild land. Too late now, we had but one direction to go and that was north. Turning back was not an option, as it would only leave me with a lifetime of regrets. I made it across the frigid water in three quick steps. That does not seem like much, but the damage that can be done in those strides is amazing.

Bending over to lace my boots, I assessed the situation. Here amid the rainforest of the Quinault River Valley all was dark, moist, and gloomy. Moss festooned every branch and trunk of the alders, every rock and shrub. Muted sunlight filtered down through the forest canopy, imparting little warmth and color to the massive sea of green around me. It was neither cold nor warm, but I managed in a long-sleeve shirt and shorts. I could not keep stopping like this and maintain that equilibrium. Time to move on through this boggy river bottom and up to tread on higher ground.

As I bent over to finish the job on my boots, my ice ax kept hitting me in the head. It seemed silly to have an ice ax at this elevation, only around five hundred feet. I better have an opportunity to use it, I thought, or I would curse the need to carry it all these miles. We set off again and immediately came upon a trough of rich, black, oozing mud. There went the shiny patina of those well-prepared boots. Through the muck and onward. Yes, this would be an adventure.

Jim and I were looking for some way to celebrate a hard year of work. He suggested this classic walk on the Olympic Peninsula of Washington. From its southern end by Lake Quinault to the northern tip by Port Angeles, a trail snaked almost fifty miles across the wilderness. Our route essentially went up one long river drainage, the Quinault, and down another, the Elwha. Trail conditions were perfect for this time of year because of the relatively low elevations; this would mean minimal travail in fighting snow cover. The high point was 3,600 feet at Low Divide—not even high by mountain standards in the Cascades. Sure, we could count on a lengthy snowy traverse at the Divide, but this would just add to the adventure and fun. Early June might sound like a late start in some parts of the country, but experience in the Northwest suggested that this was definitely not a late start. High country trails do not clear out of snow until the first part of July on the Olympic Peninsula.

We dropped Jim's car off at the north end trailhead—Whiskey Bend—and then took the better part of the day driving down to Lake Quinault campground. It was still too early in the year for many campers to be about and the campground was nearly empty—a good omen for our trip. The Elwha trail can become very crowded during the summer. It's not that Jim and I hated people; we just did not want to see anyone for several days.

For the most part, we did not bother with weather forecasts. After years of hiking in the Northwest, we had found that the best strategy was simply to decide which day we wished to venture outdoors. Then, the night before, we adjusted our packs for the most probable conditions. So long as we assumed a 100-percent probability of rain, we could not fail to win. Hiking in mist and rain was just part of the adventure. The ocean's proximity kept the humidity up and temperatures as well. It seldom became cold enough to snow. In contrast our time in the Rockies showed that it could snow at any time above 9,500 feet.

We did not have a campfire in the morning, for Jim and I were eager to be off. Still in our nongourmet days of camping, a satisfactory meal plan consisted of a stick of salami and boxes of macaroni and cheese. Jim just did not want to haul a lot of food. The plan was to supplement with fish if the opportunity came along. For my part, I was living on Fig Newtons and Snickers Bars. While not necessarily nutritious, this diet gave me plenty of calories and a full stomach. Our packs were filled to capacity, but not heavily laden with excess food. We simply intended to hike from one end of the National Park to the other.

Our route headed up the North Fork of the Quinault and the initial way was quite easy—low elevation and mild gains. The Quinault was flowing noisily along the trail for this first half-hour of the shakedown—par for the course. These long backpacking trips had assumed programmed characteristics. Lengthy planning surrounded the selection of trails consistent with time of year and number of vacation days. After immersion in topographical maps, our attention focused on meals and then finally every single piece of equipment that would be carried. The first trail mile was essential for final assessment of equipment and preparation. We might not be able to dominate nature, but we certainly were not about to have her dominate us.

Jim took the lead and set a steady pace along the wet, muddy river bottom. I was still adjusting to the load of a pack when we climbed a bit above the river and looked down into Wolf Bar Camp. It was a dark and damp camp that saw little sunlight due to the continuous canopy of dark green alders. Moss was everywhere along the trail, with ferns, grasses, and oxalis prevalent, as is common in the rainforest of the Olympic Peninsula. Jim just muttered, "Now that would be a cold camp," and kept on trudging up the trail. The morning was lengthening now, and it was easy to see that today we would have plenty of sunshine. Our spirits soared. Our only real nagging concern was Low Divide. We did not particularly want to trudge over the snow in fog or rain. If the weather would just hold for a couple of days, we would be in good shape.

We continued to hike through the dense Douglas fir and hemlock forest. The trail climbed above the river bottom, leaving the alders below. Since the Olympic Mountains are famous for precipitation, we did not have the slightest concern about the availability of water. It was everywhere.

Trees on the steep mountainsides were tall by most standards, but not by Olympic Park criteria. The Main Fork of the Quinault River begins in a stand of immense fir and hemlock. The trees are enormous at the base with impressive trunks that shout of the forest primeval. It is dizzying to walk among these giants, constantly looking up to see just how high they do reach. The entire Olympic Peninsula must have been like this once. To think of the sound and reverberations that such trees must make when they fall is a very interesting speculation. In groves such as these, an entire microclimate is created. Sheltered from the sun, nourished by decades upon decades of duff, and quenched by the liberal Pacific storms, these groves are a wonder to behold.

Early pioneers on the Olympic Peninsula had a different perspective about the beauty of these forests. It wasn't until the mid-1800s that an expedition successfully clawed its way across the peninsula primeval.

Nine

Early settlers saw the land as a vast source of economic gain if it could only be tamed. Large fisheries and virgin forests with immense fir and hemlock were the hidden treasure—not the bounty of glaciers on Mount Olympus, fragrant flower fields of subalpine country, deafening silence of the dripping forest, or spirit of the rollicking, splashing creeks. Fortunately, this land was almost too tough to tame.

Although we were not cruising through world-record trees, the trail was beautiful in its own right. It was good to replace the flat river bottom with more serious trail tread. Yet the elevation gain was quite gradual, which was just perfect considering that we were wearing packs at their maximum weight. Though not as spectacular as its Main Fork relative, the North Fork of the Quinault is blessed by a hospitable forest—something that can be enjoyed on a human level. Clearly, the differences between the main and north forks had to do with the steep hillsides and protection of the North Fork by high peaks to the west. The Main Fork of the Quinault River carries a substantially larger water flow because it encompasses a more significant drainage.

Another contrast between the Quinault River and the North Fork is access to the rivers. The Main Fork has a greater number of access points. Once you leave Wolf Bar Camp on the North Fork, the river becomes distant and diminishes in size. Before long, it becomes not an overwhelming force, but a friendly if shy companion. Your attention is drawn to the many cascades on the hillsides that glitter with fresh, crystal-clean water to quench your thirst.

We were able to hike the remainder of the day in shorts and T-shirts. In all, the experience was entirely enjoyable: gentle tread on soil with a modicum of rocks; very light breezes; temperatures in the sixty-degree range; reasonable packs; fresh water at our calling; enough variation in forest and peaks to keep our interest; and two companions who knew how to maintain a pace without constantly stopping, and who knew when to converse and when not to. We traveled in harmony with the land.

Vistas changed dramatically at the confluences of the North Fork of the Quinault, Rustler Creek (heading off to our right or northeast), and Wild Rose Creek. The valley opened in a wide expanse, allowing substantial sun to penetrate the forest. It was not clear whether this is a geological or climatic phenomenon, but I was struck by how much more open the trail and hillsides became along this route. What a contrast compared to the rainforest. We had seen similar sections of the Olympic Peninsula that mimicked this terrain and vegetation. South of Lillian Creek on the Elwha River, as well as the entire northeast rain shadow, are radically different environments compared to the lush areas around the rainforests.

We continued for another two and a half miles and enjoyed a late, leisurely lunch. As circumstances would play out, we had run into another group camped just off the trail. Here in the middle of a vast wilderness, we had chosen a site already occupied by people. This was probably more than just circumstance, having observed the same phenomenon in other locations. There seems to be certain distances that people are able to cover before they feel compelled to stop for lunch or to set up camp.

By the time Jim and I became cognizant of the presence of other people, we were virtually finished with our meal. Exchanging pleasantries, we hurried on our way—hurried to be back in the freedom of solitude. The trail seemed to gain steepness after lunch, or maybe it was a result of having already hiked some eight miles. There was a noticeable change in elevation gain that let us know the easy stuff was over. The valley began to narrow, and we looked ahead to the steep forest in which Low Divide was nestled. Occasionally we glimpsed high snowy peaks, but it was difficult to discern which peak was which.

In the latter part of the afternoon, we came upon Twelve Mile Shelter down in the shadows by the river. The site was occupied, but it did not look to be very comforting, embraced by the tumbling Quinault, all in shadows and cool. Darkness engulfed the trail. Even though we were nearing the summer solstice and days were long, filled with sunshine, and twilight delayed, there was an inescapable fact that we were walking on the east slope of very high mountains. I glanced upward but could not detect an imminent weather front. Life was good.

We only walked about another twenty minutes, or perhaps a mile, before we came to a crossing of the North Fork of the Quinault. The river was hardly recognizable compared to the start of this trip. A sixty-foot log spanned the waters and across this hand-hewn bridge, complete with a wire rail strung between wooden posts, lay a camp about twelve and one-half miles from the trailhead. And what a great camp it is! Someone had fashioned wooden seats with backs from logs. A fine fire pit was central to the site. This was a great home to arrive at after such a long day. The last fifteen minutes of hiking had provided increasing glimpses of snow within the trees. We were definitely higher in elevation and nearing Low Divide. Now was the perfect time to stop.

Nine

Jim busied himself with setting up the tent while I went to look for firewood. It was a reliable tent he had purchased some years ago, but he would never be accused of being a techie. Jim's approach to wilderness travel was very enviable. He was not obsessed with the equipment he carried and he focused on the advantages of a trail rather than its lesser qualities. Consequently, there was a discernible balance between him and the land.

Jim joined the hunt for wood. To our advantage, being early in the year, we benefited from blowdowns and remnants of a hard winter. Jim had a small blaze going in no time at all, but as with most campfires in the Northwest, it produced more smoke than flame. This fire lived down to this norm, although it removed the chill in the air. It was easy to tell that we were nearing the pass due to the colder temperature and occasional cold wind blowing down canyon. We were at just over two thousand feet in elevation. That sounds pretty puny, but in reality we were approaching the heart of a vast wilderness. This was big-time hiking, even if we were simply valley pounders instead of mountaineers.

Dinner vanished in a flash, consumed by two very hungry campers. I leaned back in my log chair. This was indeed the life we all should experience. I was tired, but not exhausted; cool, but not cold; entranced by the fire, but not hypnotized. I entered a zone of great satisfaction, becoming one with the forest and wildness.

Jim took off up the stream, ostensibly to scout and check out the possibilities for fishing. I began to doze a bit and thought back to our first backpack trip together and how far we had come. The conditions were not too dissimilar—early summer hike, lots of snow cover at elevation, and light packs.

At the end of May in the previous year, we decided to hike into Kennedy Hot Springs in the Glacier Peak Wilderness. It sounded simple enough—a six-mile trail with limited elevation gain into the heart of the wilderness. Esther, his wife, went along for the trip. She hated backpacking. The greatest moment for her was turning around. No one, absolutely no one, could keep up with Esther when we returned, especially if the way was downhill. She could fly with her short little legs pumping along. The day that we hiked into the Kennedy Hot Springs started out perfectly clear. A brilliant sun was blazing with occasional high clouds while a gentle breeze filtered through the dark fir trees. The trail was snow free at the start and relatively dry despite recent rains. I was all ready to go with my super-light gear. No tent for me. I would erect a tarp. No heavy bag for me. I carried a scaled-down model. No rain suit for me. I would carry only a poncho in view of the fine weather.

The trail began above the White Chuck River at about the same elevation where we now camped in the Olympic Park Wilderness— 2,300 feet. Down to the west of us flowed the White Chuck River, agitated at this time of year with white water and frothing swells. Starting down the trail, we looked to the peaks surrounding us—white with snow at their upper exposed elevations. Trees concealed snow smothering the ground. The weather was quite warm—somewhere in the mid-sixty-degree range—with wispy clouds floating overhead. Mare's tails are not a good sign, but when you are in the Northwest, you simply go on your scheduled trip. We took several photos of the surrounding mountains and headed off for the springs.

The trail was gentle at first and well defined. It certainly saw considerable traffic and there were even five vehicles parked at the trailhead on this early date. Things went predictably for the first mile. The river roared. Esther complained about her pack. The trees were big and getting bigger.

There is truly nothing as impressive as virgin Northwest forest. Huge Douglas fir, cedar, and hemlock tower over the trail, beautiful in their symmetry and scent. Various branches blown down during winter litter the forest floor, and there is normally limited undergrowth. Happy to be walking through this paradise after almost seven months of perpetual cloudy and gray skies, I reveled in this sunny day in the woods.

Patches of snow began to appear within the forest. Suddenly we reached the snowline, walking on snow up to two feet deep. Over the course of the next three miles this base would increase up to about five feet. Due to the intense radiation, my sunglasses provided minimal protection, and even then I squinted. Sun-melted snow turned into a difficult mush in which to gain a purchase. We had more elevation to climb, made that much more difficult owing to the vast snowfields. Our route was not difficult to follow because parties had cross-country skied into Kennedy Hot Springs at some point during the winter and spring, leaving tracks behind them.

So the passage went. Esther gave us lots of grief for the conditions. However, my light pack and the bright sun kept me buoyant despite her recriminations. At about four and a half miles we came upon a hundred-yard landslide where the trail and hillside had recently washed into the White Chuck River. Past rains and heavy snowmelt had saturated the hillside, letting it slough down into the river. We picked our way carefully across the slide, but I could not help to think that it could let loose again at any minute. Jim verbalized this very thought a few seconds later.

Back on solid snow, we entered the shallow bowl containing Kennedy Hot Springs. At the edge of the bowl we had to cross a slight creek drainage coming down off Glacier Peak. I eyed this drainage suspiciously, given the devastation we had just crossed. A few years later an ice dam high up on a glacier let go and destroyed this creek while inundating the campground. It obliterated the area where we would sleep tonight.

Jim set up his tent while I fiddled with my tarp tent. Once his tent was standing he unrolled his mattresses and bags so that Esther could take a nap. While Jim jumped into the horrible vomit-colored Kennedy Hot Springs, I continued to work on my tarp. I guess I should have given this more thought at home. The tarp tent worked perfectly on level, dry soil, but it was a disaster to set up in the snow given the lack of secure anchors. I tried all of the tricks for burying pegs and stretching guy lines. It just was not working.

A three-sided log shelter remained standing by the ranger station. Gruesome with lots of filth everywhere, the shelter was made from small-diameter logs in the eight-inch range with a sloping roof to the rear. This shelter had seen plenty of use over the decades and was nearing its final days. The dirt floor, however, was dry, which meant that the roof still worked. This was hard to believe looking up at the cedar shakes, which had daylight showing in several places. Bits of plant life were evident in the recesses where boots could not squash them. A wood rack for sleeping graced the northern wall and several slats were missing, but it was serviceable. Appearance would not matter all that much once it turned dark. I staked my claim to this ancient heritage site—this would be better than sleeping on the snow.

No sooner had I made my claim than the skies began to cloud up and the sun lost its intensity. A chill descended on the site and given the massive snowfields and glaciers towering above us, I am surprised that it was no colder. That's the magic of the Northwest. The high humidity and low elevations tend to keep things temperate. We used the snow-free front of the shelter as a cook site and prepared a frugal meal. Esther was appalled that Jim would bring so little food. Thankfully, I had brought plenty of survival food—Snickers Bars. We were so tired from slogging through snow that when finished with dinner we went to bed, but it took a long time for twilight to leave since we were well along to the summer solstice.

My lightweight modified mummy bag was open at the top. This feature allowed me to save weight, but as I learned that night, it carried an expensive price tag of limited protection for my head, where over 50 percent of all body heat is lost. Actually, I was less concerned about this problem when the first raindrops began to hit the shelter's roof. Yes, we would test the theory that the roof worked.

I would like to say that after sufficient rain fell to confirm the worthiness of the roof, I fell into deep slumber. I would like to say that, but I cannot. I am not certain whether I remained awake because a mouse ran over my sleeping bag and face or because of the thought that more rain would surely cause the water-sodden slope below camp to crash into the White Chuck River. In any case, it was a long cool night without much sleep, leaving the impression that I was out of balance with the wilderness. I had not thought carefully enough about how I would fit into Glacier Peak and Kennedy Hot Springs—how I would blend with the mountain rather than thinking that the mountain would blend into me.

Mornings after a traumatic night always seem to be reassuring. This morning was not. I roused Esther and Jim in the belief that we needed to get the heck out of there as fast as we could. Jim agreed. This set Esther in motion and the miles flew by. How could it take only 40 percent of the time to hike out that it took to hike in? Shortly we were back at the car and headed back to Seattle. I sat in the back, mentally listing the faux pas that would not be repeated soon.

The campfire rose up in a bright blaze as the wood began to dry and burn more noisily—brighter and more efficiently. I snapped out of my stupor as Jim came back to camp. "We will be on snow for the rest of the way to Low Divide. That will be about five miles." My mind raced. Was this déjà vu? Was I back at Glacier Peak? I took stock of the situation. For one thing, I had brought along a proper mummy bag rated to zero degrees. I also had a down parka and shells to repel moisture. I carried a stash of extra food knowing that Jim required less than I did. Then again, I would be sharing the tent with Jim. Early lessons had transformed themselves into better preparation. Still, that old edge hung in the air. Tomorrow we would have to get going early to avoid a sun-softened snowy trail, and to beat any bad weather to the pass. I slept like a rock.

Up very early the next morning, we were soon on our way—no morning fire or lingering breakfast this time. I had a delicious meal of pop tarts and hot chocolate—perfect because the temperature was very cool. Dressed in long wool pants with a wool shirt and parka, I prepared for the pass.

Within ten minutes we were on constant snow as the trail wound up to the pass. Route finding along the way was easy, for other parties had already broken the snow either in cross-country skiing or post holing when walking. The sky had a tinge of overcast, which drove both of us onward since we wanted to put the pass behind us and to find out what might be waiting on the other side. Jim led the way again with his ice ax at the ready, using it for support as a walking assist. The ice ax had the advantage of allowing us to chop steps if needed, and it was far better than a ski pole or hiking staff in the vertical terrain of the Cascades.

The trail held to the east side of the small valley leading to Low Divide. We were in small fir about forty feet high. Colors were almost absent due to high clouds, ever-present dark green fir, snow cover, and the early morning hours, but sun would occasionally break through the gloom and trees to light a glade. Down to our immediate west the Quinault flowed silently, muffled by snow and trees. It was cold, near freezing, but not threatening. We had enough experience, equipment, and physical conditioning to turn this challenge into a pleasant memory, and I relaxed. Free of worry, I felt at harmony with the vast wild lands surrounding me—we were a part of, rather than apart from, the wilderness.

Little streamlets flowed down the hill from the east, hinting at the beauty to come later in the year. At one larger creek, a wooden foot-bridge had been constructed to avoid the mud and the muck. Sun was shining merrily on the pure water flowing in freshets toward the Quinault and eventually the sea. I had moved into the lead at this point and just did not see it coming. The bridge was covered in a form of black ice—or bridge ice—that was not readily visible. About two feet above the stream, the bridge was just high enough to allow cold air to circulate and to create ice. It was leaning downhill to the west and thus my feet went sliding out from under me—a rude awakening and warning that this was, after all, big-time wilderness. My ice ax prevented me from making a total fool of myself, and luckily, no damage was done.

After two hours of fighting slippery snow and the growing sense that for every step forward we were sliding back one, an indentation in the terrain ahead suggested that we might be nearing the pass. The trail was beginning to level off a bit, but we had been in these situations many times before. You reach a false summit and then try to remotivate yourself for another significant amount of elevation gain.

We entered a thinning stand of fir trees and then all of a sudden there we were in a clearing free of snow, with views into an enormous drainage to the north and toward towering peaks to the west. It was Low Divide.

Triumphant, we made our way to a clear patch of dirt and greenery in the warm sun. Jim and I both sensed the pleasure that only comes after hard work and investment. What a grand feeling this was to have conquered the mid-point (in elevation terms at 3,600 feet) of this trail. It was literally all downhill from this point.

Packs were dropped as we decided to have an impromptu brunch. Jim fired up the stove and we enjoyed a warm cup of soup along with biscuits. This was a stunning scene at which to stop. Clouds had parted and we knew that even if the remainder of the trip was rainy, we would be able to slog it out to the car. We had reached a major milestone that foretold a wonderful walk through the woods over the vast tree-filled wilderness at our feet.

Views to the north were captivating given the inspiring snow and glaciers on high peaks to the northwest. We were too low in elevation and too close to the mountain to see Mount Olympus and much of the Bailey Range, but we knew they were there. Surrounding peaks spoke of winter that still lingered despite the fact that the snow and glaciers sparkled in the sun to the point that it hurt to look at them. Meanwhile, to the direct north was a distant view toward Hurricane Ridge and the Straits of Juan de Fuca. We could see the intermediate mountains to be navigated along the Elwha River before reaching our destination. The view northward foretold a serious wilderness still to cross.

Immediately north were the lakes of Low Divide—Lake Mary and Lake Margaret—still covered with ice and snow. The snow depth at the divide was approximately three feet on the level. We knew that the lakes were out there somewhere, but they were very difficult to discern given the drifted snow. Discussing the need for extreme caution in negotiating these lakes after my fall on the wooden bridge, the last thing we needed was to fall through the ice into one of the lakes.

We finished our meal while being besieged by chipmunks. With a final bite to eat, we reassembled our packs and headed toward the Elwha River Valley. My boots were soaked through with water. I had taken them off when we stopped and donned dry tennis shoes. Now it was painful to put the wet, cold boots back on.

After Lake Mary and Lake Margaret the trail just seemed to disappear as we stood looking down into the Elwha River Valley. There were approximately twenty-nine miles left to cover before we reached the car at Whiskey Bend, and the trail would skirt the Elwha River the entire way. This magnificent, powerful river flows from the glaciers and highlands of Mount Olympus. At this time of the year the river was a dark blue-green. It did not resemble rivers that typically flow from glacier sources. Of course, many tributaries flow into the Elwha and dilute the typical glacial melt appearance.

The Elwha was formerly known for its rich habitat for salmon. A dam by Whiskey Bend stopped the migration of the salmon in exchange for virtually nothing in the way of power or flood control. The good news is that current debates are ongoing about removing the dam and returning the Elwha to its wild state. This river needs to be set free. Walk its upper reaches and know that this fine watercourse should never have been subjugated by human whims. Standing near the headwaters of the Elwha and looking down its long course, you have a much better perspective of the cruel desecration created by the dam. This wild country deserves to be free from our touch. The dam only accentuates how out of balance our society is with nature.

Jim and I gazed down into the valley looking for our next camp—Chicago Camp—about three miles from Low Divide. In the course of the next two hours we would plummet 1,500 feet down to the Elwha. Since the trail simply vanished in the snow and trees, we were trying to sight the best direction to head toward camp, but it would be difficult to get lost without the trail. The Elwha should remain on our left (west); head north. Thus, we were not the least anxious dropping down into the forest. Our ice axes proved useful in the mad dash to low ground because the way was very steep in the dense, snow-covered woods.

Each of us took a few more slides on snow and mud than we would have liked to under the conditions. Sliding, however, was not the worst problem. The rotten snow under and around logs and trees made it possible to plunge up to our hips if we were not careful. This morning's graceless fall remained fresh in my mind, so I was extremely careful about placing my feet and making certain I had solid purchase before shifting weight. Just as this exertion with a full pack began to lose its fun and Jim was sharing a few expletives, the snow cover stopped just like that.

We stepped out of the snow and looked around. There directly below us was firm trail tread. Once again we had witnessed the snow-line phenomenon—this line is consistent on a gradient and gradually rises as temperatures warm up. Fairly constant rates of melting occur to produce this definitive line. Perhaps we were just lucky in finding the trail directly below us. More likely, the trail just switches back and forth from the bottom of the valley up to the divide. This was definitely the case for the remaining drop down to the valley floor. We simply walked down a series of switchbacks until the way leveled out. We had arrived at the Elwha.

The river was definitely strong, but not overwhelmingly large at this point. We were able to cross it with ease on enormous tree trunks, but our explorations were soon forgotten in the pursuit of Chicago Camp. Since this is a primary departure point for climbers headed to Mount Olympus, we expected to be sharing the camp with many others. When we arrived no one was in camp. It would remain this way for the night. By now it was over twenty-four hours since we had seen anyone, and it would be another twenty-four hours and seventeen miles before we would run into other people. This was truly a wilderness experience that enabled us to blend back into nature. Free of people and the trappings of civilization, we regained equilibrium with the earth.

Jim and I walked through heavy forest until we glided into Chicago Camp. The site possessed an inherent serenity and beauty that only a camp miles from civilization can hold. With a few boisterous climbers running around the place in summer, the atmosphere must be altogether different from what Jim and I experienced.

We set up the tent and Jim headed off to fish. There still was plenty of afternoon left, so I went about finding firewood in order to get the fire going. Given how busy this camp is in summer, virtually no wood was to be found anywhere. The forest had been picked clean. On a previous trip Jim's father had taught us how to go under a tree's canopy to find seasoned dry twigs that can be used to start fires. I was able to add this fire starter to slightly larger pieces that had fallen during the winter. For the really big logs I went down to the river, where pieces of stranded driftwood are inevitably to be found. Before long I had a wonderful cloud of smoke heading skyward, but little blaze.

I pulled on my long pants and settled down around the fire. These were rich moments. Here we were in the middle of the park, with utter silence except for the sounds of nature—the rushing Elwha, an occasional birdcall, the wind through the firs, and a pleasant crackle of the fire. In the silence I thought about how much I loved the outdoors. Everything fit together with fantastic harmony and balance. Beauty was all around if you just looked at it. The sun streamed through the smoke and boughs of the trees, creating a magical curtain of light and form.

It is amazing, the things humans can do. Here we were with a few pounds of nylon, feathers, and aluminum, yet we had all we needed to survive—tent, sleeping bag, and clothes. Miles from civilization, we were completely at home and secure. As my thoughts unfolded, a doe came silently to the edge of the camp and wandered past the fire. I called to her quietly. Her ears perked at my sound—one ear going up and the other going down. She stared at me for a while, and then carefully picked her way back into the forest. Her soft brown fur reflected the sheen of a new season. Her movements were so graceful. Yes, there was abundant life here after all. You just had to slow down long enough to observe its presence; once in harmony with the earth, its bounty would be revealed. Jim and I had been on the go from the moment that we started. It was just a matter of settling down and becoming one with the land.

Well past dinnertime, Jim was nowhere to be found. Should I go looking for him? This is always the problem for those left in camp. Fishermen stay out longer than they intend because they do not have the luck they anticipated. Several times I started up the trail, but held back. Along the Elwha the forest and brush were very dense. I would have great difficulty walking along the river without concerted effort. Jim may well have walked a half-mile up the trail before heading over to the river. He may have explored a side stream. Best to wait. In time—a long time—he showed up in camp with nothing for his efforts. Good thing we were not relying on him for dinner. He was soaked up to his waist and hurriedly changed his clothes. He had fallen into the river and just saved himself from going in completely. That made one close call for each of us—we were even.

Rambling along Rainforest Paths

Night closed in with a vengeance. Down here in the valley with massive Mount Olympus and the Bailey Range obscuring the sun, darkness came early. We sat around the smoky fire talking about our commitment to mountains, wilderness, the earth, and the direction we were headed for the future. We vowed to stay connected with the wild in one form of pastime or another.

As we broke camp the next morning, our conversation drifted to how lucky we had been relative to the weather. Here was a third day that had started without rain, mist, or heavy cloud. True to our habit, we did not have a fire that morning, with the thought of making as many miles as might be possible before the day ended. Hot water was boiling in no time to provide for oatmeal and breakfast bars. Our efficiency had increased greatly, and soon we were headed down the trail.

The morning presented a happy combination of walking challenges and surprises. While the trail was very gradually losing elevation, we were constantly gaining and losing elevation to avoid this downed tree, that ravine, or this stream. The way was generally free of obstacles, but being this early in the season, a number of trees had fallen down across the trail. Only two were substantial monsters that left us wondering what the crash must have been like when they toppled. Scents of fresh fir and disturbed soil were combined in an aromatic elixir. Devastation to other lesser trees and shrubs was impressive—everyone gives up something when big trees fall down, and now the battle was on for which tree would dominate the new supply of sun. Detouring around these behemoths and some of the lesser fallen comrades required either going around the base or scrambling up over the massive trunks. The Park Service would require some impressive handsaws, and probably a team of mules, in order to remove these specimens from the trail.

After several miles we came to the rushing torrent of Buckinghorse Creek. There was no established bridge, only a fallen log high above the rushing stream. Fortunately, the sun was shining on our challenge, and we took time to plot a course across the log. Out came the ice axes with their metal spikes to help stabilize our crossing. It was a nervous moment inching across the Douglas fir with its pealing bark and spray-covered smooth inner bark. Focus on each step. Do not think about what might happen if you slip. Over onto the other side and breathe a sigh of relief.

By now the Elwha River was growing much larger. It commanded respect. We could see where enormous trees had been moved in earlier floods. The river itself was much more powerful than back at Chicago Camp. Each little rivulet and side stream was adding to its power. I just hoped that the topographical maps were right in indicating that we did not have to cross the river. That would have been a challenge that I would not want to try. Sure, there were occasional giant trees down that spanned this impressive river, but they were few and far between. If we did have to cross, it would be a very tense proposition, looking down into the swirling, frigid Elwha. It was a great place for salmon, but not for people.

We strolled along, making progress without overtly discussing where we would spend the night. Several times we passed camps or trails leading to side camps, but we never did venture down them, nor did we see a soul. Today, these camps are prohibited owing to problems with black bears. An eight-mile stretch of the Elwha has camping restrictions to manage the bear-people interface. Habituated bears eventually become dead bears. This closure adds a real challenge to backpackers, who must now carefully plan mileage and campsites.

The morning continued to be sunny and warm, and we could not ask for better hiking weather as the sun had burned off the early chill. What once had been the low forties at Chicago Camp now gave way to the high fifties as we approached Hayes River Guard Station. This log structure seemed impressive at first glance—a log shelter in the middle of the wilderness—but on closer inspection it was clear who had the upper hand on the peninsula. It looked frail in comparison to the forest we had negotiated to this point, but at the same time it served as a good reminder that we were alone only because of the time of the season. Another week and the trail would be inundated with scout troops and youth out of school.

The Elwha was less visible along some stretches of the trail owing to groves of large trees, flooding devastation that had rerouted the trail just a bit higher on the mountainside, and variations in the topography that demanded gentle gradients for trail construction. Jim and I just kept walking. As we made progress down the river, the valley began to open up, and we could see mountain ridges that were familiar from previous hikes and camping trips up the Elwha. It was a distinct shock when we finally recognized just how far we had traveled at lunch. Here it was early in the afternoon and we had completed more than twelve miles. We stopped to discuss where we should camp. I suggested Mary Falls, a day's journey up the Elwha at about nine miles.

Rambling along Rainforest Paths

We just kept on walking with little thought to speed or destination. It felt good to be on the trail, and by now we were in great shape. Our packs had lightened up considerably as the food was going fast. The next major structure was Elkhorn Guard Station, but Jim did not even hesitate when we came upon it. By midafternoon we cruised into the camping area at Mary Falls and ran into the first people that we had seen in almost forty-eight hours.

Although we had not intended to set speed records, our first and third days registered significant mileage. This had nothing to do with unique abilities, only the gentle gradient and our commitment to cover the miles methodically. Still, we felt special about the accomplishment and reveled in our conditioning. We set up our final camp down by the river and proceeded to fish.

A sunny day had now grown quite hot, and exposure out on the river only made the temperature feel higher. I took the time to wash my clothes before swimming cautiously in the Elwha's eddies and trying to catch fish in a deep blue-green pool. This cavernous depression was perhaps twenty yards wide in an oblong shape. The water must have been on order of twenty feet deep in the pool. I could see the power of the river at this point and knew that it was in total control. This pool deserved to have salmon in it: a harmony of fish and river.

The afternoon passed uneventfully with few high clouds. I sat out on the sandbars and river rock speculating on what the Elwha must look like to leave these huge trees and rocks behind. Was it sudden storms, or the height of snowmelt that brought the river up these levels? I did not want to know. That would be an awesome spectacle. I have seen the Main Fork of the Quinault after a heavy thunderstorm—itself a rare occurrence—and it was not pretty. There is one whole lot of country emptying into these rivers. Still, given the constant battering of heavy runoff, it is amazing that more damage is not done. The loam of the forest duff must act like a great sponge, meting out slow measures of runoff to prevent large-scale devastation.

Day was edging toward evening, and we were beginning to prepare for dinner when an uninvited guest came into camp. A young man came over to talk. He was quite skinny and carried a day sack with some goods. The fellow asked for directions and inquired about whether it was possible to hike across the mountains. He pulled a roadmap, of all things, out of his pack and asked for advice. I was dumbfounded. Jim simply pointed out where we were and where this fellow would travel.

Then the lad brought out a loaf of white bread—his only food. Now I got it. He was angling for an invitation to dinner. Unfortunately, we were seriously low on food ourselves. Neither Jim nor I took the bait, nor did we move a muscle toward showing what we had for dinner or preparing dinner with him around.

Our unwanted guest lingered for what seemed like hours. At long last he bade us farewell and took off—up the trail? I have no way of knowing which way he went. No wonder people get into trouble out in the wilderness. They must think that convenience stores are just around the bend, or that the Park Service will come to rescue their sorry souls should they get in trouble. As Jim and I had just found out, you can go days without seeing anyone. Rescue may be too late by the time help reaches you. We turned our attention to dinner and thoroughly enjoyed what we had left—which was not much.

Rising early the next morning, we finished our last breakfast. Food was now a major issue—nothing was left. The good news was the weather. Once again we dodged the storm bullet, but I expected as such. The trail from Whiskey Bend must be located in an apparent rain shadow. Up the grade from Lillian River the hillside has shrubs that are much like manzanita covering the hills in Southern California. We had plenty of opportunity to appreciate this dry portion of the trail climbing up from Mary Falls Camp and skirting the Elwha high on the mountainside. Here the forest was sparse and trees stunted, but once we turned the corner and dropped down into Lillian River the entire ecosystem changed to lush Olympic Park greenery, and then thinned out on the final descent toward Whiskey Bend.

The route out from Lillian River is lined with side trails to former homesteads that the Park Service has tried to preserve. Cougar Mike's Cabin and Humes Ranch testify to hardy souls drawn to this land who carved out a living in what then must have seemed like a desolate place. Our technology allows us to tame the wilderness and deliver a form of adventure that cannot begin to approximate what the early settlers experienced in their effort to survive a very challenging land fraught with potential dangers. There must have been much less time available for appreciating nature as Jim and I had just done over the last four days.

The Elwha was far below us as we reached the car and trailhead. It is a magnificent river that imparted only some of its personality and soul with us while we walked its length. The Elwha was forever changing color and consistency; once frothy and white, now it was green and serene. Jim and I felt honored to have shared these days with the Quinault and Elwha, having achieved balance with the vast and sweeping wilderness from which they sprang.

Before we realized it, the trip was over. Jim took a final photo of me standing against the trail sign announcing the 48.5 miles to the North Fork Ranger Station. We loaded our packs and smelly bodies into the car and sat down on an upholstered seat for a return to unreality. We did not have to wait very long. As Jim warmed up the car, he suddenly set the brake, got out, and went around the side. The crowning welcome-back had occurred. Jim filled the car with gas in Port Angeles before driving it the few miles to the trailhead. In the interim, some kind soul had come along and stolen the gas from his tank. Welcome home, hearty adventurers.

❊ ❊ ❊

A long backpack across the Olympic Peninsula presents both a challenge and an opportunity. On one hand, preparation for the journey requires serious attention to equipment that will be used to succeed in an endeavor through distant wilderness far from easily accessible help. On the other hand, such a trip also offers the opportunity to achieve balance with nature as civilization is left behind and a more natural pace envelops life. The challenge creates the possibility not only to reflect in deeply meaningful ways about the earth, but also to achieve balance with natural rhythms and life that is free from human convention.

In crossing the Olympic Peninsula from south to north on a frequently used footpath, we inevitably reached the serene campsite known as Chicago Camp. The blessings of timing were upon us because the season was too early for mountain climbers to have captured the site. No one was around. There, deep in the wilderness, we were able to achieve balance and grace in wildness. Having been on the trail long enough to sufficiently disconnect from normal urban patterns and activities, Jim and I experienced harmony with a vast wilderness formed of mountain ranges, glaciers, virgin forests, swift flowing rivers and streams, meadows, and ice-choked lakes. Yet, on exiting, we were affronted by a dam on the very wilderness river we had come to know so well—a dam that is decidedly disharmonious with the earth and wildness; a dam that symbolizes fruitless efforts to control nature.

Nine

This wilderness tale serves as an allegory of an attempt to walk in harmony on this earth. Distracted by the superficial and ephemeral in our culture while being lured by what some see as the pornography of materialism, it is very hard to break free and develop a harmonious relationship with nature. Even when we achieve balance, plenty of intrusions are waiting to throw us off track. A culture that deeply loves the earth must be persistent and passionate—committed to living harmoniously with the wild, dedicated to its preservation, and wise enough to avert presumptions about human control over nature.

Everything
Is
Connected

10

The Red Road

In the far northwest corner of New Mexico, an intriguing high-desert canyon contains the remnants of a past civilization. Left behind are many artifacts and signs of habitation, but few definitive answers for precise interpretation. In a shallow river course at the base of sage- and grass-covered mesas sits an apparently lonely outpost of intricate sandstone construction. Weathered over the last ten centuries, Chaco Canyon no longer rings to the footsteps of a bustling community, the laughter and cries of children, or the commotion surrounding a magnificent architectural accomplishment. A throaty call of ravens echoes within the remnants of stone walls that remain as silent sentinels over the sacred site. Lonely wails from prowling coyotes drift down from the mesas in the chill evening air. Rabbits freeze in rapt attention to the mournful hoots of wise and stealthy old owls.

Chaco Canyon once was a bustling community, full of life and vigor. But, somewhere along the road to its success, decline began. Authorities argue that it was drought, religious decay, or catastrophic disease that led to Chaco's demise. David E. Stuart offers a compelling vision of Chaco Canyon's rise and fall in *Anasazi America*. According to Stuart, Chaco experienced an economic phenomenon of growth, surplus, and market diversification. Plentiful rainfall encouraged rapid community growth and crop abundance. Trade routes were established to capitalize on this largess, creating an infrastructure of roads and societal relations not previously known. However, all of this innovation and economic affluence came crashing to the ground as weather moderated and crops diminished.

Chaco Canyon represents yet another example of naturally occurring interconnections. Hunting and gathering activities by native peoples were only the prelude to a period of dramatic growth fueled by a serendipitous combination of increasing rainfall and more sophisticated knowledge about corn, beans, squash, and other crops. Wild game and indigenous food sources did not have the capacity to create population revolution or cultural innovation. Nonetheless, as new farming technology coincided with other important preconditions—above-average rainfall, availability of seeds and food crops, innovations in crop and dwelling infrastructure, trade outlets to capitalize on crop surpluses—a renaissance bloomed over the plateau and Chaco culture flourished.

Nature personifies the concept of interconnectivity. When one element in the natural scheme of things is disrupted, many subsequent perturbations unfold. In a secluded mountain ravine, a newly fallen Alaskan cedar causes a slight southerly diversion in a stream and subsequently protects the roots of a Douglas fir that was slowly drowning in an abundance of excess water. Farther up the ravine, disease in a stand of aspen opens the forest canopy and a profusion of lupine and other plant life rises in exaltation. Deer feed purposefully on the new bounty of food and produce more offspring, which lure mountain lions into the previously empty canyon. The cycle of life continues, because for every change in the ecosystem a corresponding reaction occurs: everything is connected to everything else.

A culture that deeply loves the earth acknowledges the pervasiveness of connectedness within the world. Such a culture exercises great care relative to the role of humans within the circle of life to ensure that our progress is not detrimental to the rest of life on this home— this earth—that we share. The preservation of wildness becomes a barometer against which the progress of civilization is measured.

❁ ❁ ❁

Thump. Thump. Thump. Thump. Was it the persistent, measured beat of the drum or was it my heart? Reality mixed with illusion, and I had no way of knowing which was which. For the moment I was contending with the bath of perspiration drenching my body and intense heat seemingly determined to broil me alive. This was definitely an adventure of body, mind, and spirit, yet a path that seemed so familiar. Inside this humble cathedral, the experience blended the best and the worst. The best was feeling humility before the Creator while the worst was a tangible premonition of a fatal medical crisis.

The initial round of my first *inipi*, or sweat lodge, ceremony was only a small step in learning my Red Road—Native ways (as opposed to the sobriety program for Native Americans)—and a moment in which I saw the beauty of an alternative form of worship. The shaman ordered me to move from the back of the lodge to the front by the door. As cool air poured past my drenched skin, the refreshing gift calmed my fears and gave me the courage to carry on. Continuing with his lessons, we had a brief reprieve from the heat, steam, and dark.

Ten

Several Native American friends at work invited me to share with them in an inipi ceremony. My friend Alistair had entered the sweat lodge first—he had a long history of spiritual exploration around the world. "Come try it. You will like it," he chided me. Alistair has a great flair for life, and he underscored that this sort of opportunity does not always materialize at the convenience of your schedule.

In Western society a romanticized view prevails that American Indians are one with nature. For many Indians their connection with nature and Mother Earth forms the very definition of being. Yet, for others, the traditional ways and beliefs are foreign, beat out of them by early European invaders or Bureau of Indian Affairs policies, supplanted by secular materialism and the obsessions of modern society. Many non-Natives are intrigued by this spirituality espousing a vibrant relationship with nature and uplifting the sacredness of all life—not just human life.

Mother Earth and Father Sun form central ingredients of a complex animistic belief system that anthropologists and theologians have tried for years to understand. While indigenous peoples have imparted a great wealth of knowledge about religious practices, much still remains a mystery. I will never ever fully understand the religious beliefs of Native Americans, or even a single tribe. I cannot know what it is like to have a deep sense of genetic connectedness to a small tribe of indigenous family and friends. I cannot easily experience the sense of bewilderment, confusion, and anger that Indians feel when interfacing with dominant society. My relatives have not passed down centuries of ritual, myth, and culture about their experiences and what life is all about. I can only begin to appreciate but a very small portion of the inherent beauty of their spiritual practices.

Despite these realities, there is substantial merit in trying to understand and embrace the best parts of a philosophy of life that reveres nature and accepts the universality of living harmoniously with all life and the earth. Spiritual views that render humans as equal with other life possess a compelling attraction. Creatures of this planet do not have any less right to a full life than us. They were not made for our idle fancy, amusement, and entertainment, or for us to dominate. Each of us, no matter how hardened and lost to the superficiality of contemporary human-centered life, has the innate ability to appreciate and seek out a harmonious balance with other people, animals, and the planet that we share. For all of us to survive on this planet, we desperately need to regain this intimacy of harmony with nature and Mother Earth.

The Red Road

Although intrigued by the Native American ceremonies, I had no interest in becoming an Indian—a "wannabe." But when Alistair mentioned the inipi ceremony, the time was right to investigate further. He offered to attend with me and briefly described the ceremony. It seemed simple enough. Anxious about the ceremony, I did not know exactly what to expect, nor did I know the participants. Nonetheless, there I was walking into the shaman's backyard, circling a roaring fire, the altar, and the lodge.

Who were these people? It was difficult for me to see in the dark. The flames of the fire only showed passing glimpses of their faces. Most could claim Native American heritage. A few were descendants from Mayan Indians. I was from Grossmont, California.

Per instruction, we circled the sweat lodge and ended up at a dirt altar in front of the lodge, slightly set back from the fire. Offering tobacco to the spirits of the fire and the superheated rocks, I tried to form a coherent prayer, but my mind was racing.

A gift of tobacco was presented to the shaman, who welcomed me to the circle and prepared for our ceremony. The celebrants sitting close to the fire chatted among themselves. It was a very cold November night, and the fire felt good. Little did I realize that soon I would covet the cool air.

Word was passed among the men to enter the lodge. Soon everyone had stripped down to bathing trunks. I carried a towel with me to keep scalding steam from my head and back, but no one else seemed to need this crutch. A line was formed, and we began to enter the inipi lodge. I tried to mimic the others as best I could, but I did not understand all of the rituals and connections. Some turned to the four corners with their hands in prayer. More than one bent down and kissed Mother Earth before entering the lodge. I scooted into the cramped tortoiseshell-shaped lodge. In the center was a fire pit into which the red-hot rocks would be brought. I tried to sit with my legs folded in a sort of lotus fashion. Alistair sat next to me in a show of—support? Stupidity? I really wondered.

The shaman asked for rocks to be brought into the lodge, and suddenly my world changed from the predictable to a superheated cloak of warmth.

Out of respect for the participants and the culture, I will not reveal the specifics of the ceremony within the lodge. Suffice it to say that by the end of the first round, I was ready for a very quick exit when a sense of compassion flooded the lodge. Directed to sit by the door, the shaman explained how it might be necessary to lie down on Mother Earth to avoid the direct assault of the heat. It was suggested that I focus on prayer; prayer to the grandmothers and grandfathers—the rocks—to elevate my consciousness beyond concern for myself.

It was not a pretty sight, but in the end, with their help, I managed to complete four rounds of praying, cleansing, chanting, and petitioning. I did not experience a serious allergic reaction to herbs that were used, and I did not stroke out from the heat and smoke. But I did go through one of those defining moments in life and left with a better understanding of some things about life.

On returning home I was filthy but elated. Steam and the earthen floor of the lodge conspired to render even the tidiest person dirty beyond imagination. Dirt was everywhere, but it just did not seem to matter. Carefully placing a towel on the seat of my car to protect the upholstery from damage, I drove off into the night. Everything took on a new glow as I drove through the darkened streets of the barrio. At home it was time for a long shower. Amazingly, the smoke of the fire and cedar incense had soaked through the pores of my skin. I could still smell the remnants from the inipi ceremony the next day—a deeper purification than I realized.

I found other opportunities to participate in inipi ceremonies. Sensitive to a lack of seasoning to the heat and steam, I tried to judge the needs of others and the role that I could best play in the ceremony. If there were many participants in a sweat, I usually requested the honor of "pulling rocks" by performing the role of "fireman"—one who pulls the rocks from the fire and delivers the rocks to the lodge. The fireman makes certain that the fire is maintained to keep the temperature of the grandfathers and grandmothers at a maximum. Typically, the keeper of the fire does not join the ceremony within the lodge.

Since shamans vary in their rituals, it is just as common for all the heated rocks to be brought into the lodge as it is to have the rocks equally divided among the rounds. The fireman closes the lodge door and opens it at the end of each round of prayer. In many respects, this role is one of service, of giving, to others. This seemed particularly fitting for me since I was for all intents and purposes an interloper. However, I was never made to feel that I was intruding, or that my heritage somehow denigrated the ceremonies. Perhaps there was talk about this very issue among this circle, but it never reached my ears.

The power of the inipi ceremony was startling even for a fireman. I remember quite clearly this magic one evening when the rounds were extended over their normal course and there was much praying and chanting among the large number of celebrants. The third round was ready to begin after I delivered more grandfathers into the lodge. The door was shut, and I tended the fire, making certain that the rocks had not cooled and coals were neatly covering them. I could hear the prayers of the circle inside. Often the petitions were in Native languages—Navajo, Comanche, Lakota, Apache—which created a special spell. Everything was at peace. I reflected on how the members of this circle were extremely poor, without many of the givens that we take for granted—comfortable salary, health insurance, home, savings accounts, pension plan, and so forth. Yet, they showed me the highest respect and friendship and made the effort to incorporate me in this special part of their lives.

Praying by the fire with a melodic chant being sung as a backdrop, I was flooded with the beauty of their humility. These were fine people. They showed grand qualities that well-educated, rich, and worldly people seldom display. Here I was in one of the most economically deprived parts of the city sharing in praise to the Great Spirit, to the Creator. There was nothing false, fake, or phony about this church. It may have lacked carpeted floors and stained glass windows, but the sincerity of belief and faith were immeasurably beyond that found in most chapels, synagogues, or cathedrals. Inside the lodge the supplicants asked for forgiveness, strength, courage, healing, empowerment, and other requests appropriate to their lives and circumstances. I was filled with love and respect for these people.

Precisely at this moment the futility of materialism came crashing home—so shallow, so meaningless, so unrewarding and so detrimental to living a spirit-filled life. The clarity of my vision was extraordinary—it was as though I had left my body and was looking down on myself. Profoundly humbled and embarrassed, I realized I had been living for the wrong things—indeed, I had been living for things. Inside the lodge were people who had virtually nothing, but who shared a far greater relationship with their god than did I. I will never forget that moment, and my pledge to use the vision to maintain a better balance in life.

A powerful lesson on the interconnectedness of everything occurred one night when tending a fire honoring those who were in the mountains on a vision quest. Participants in a vision quest are placed on a mountain for four days of fasting and prayer in search of a vision from the Great Spirit. A perpetual fire is started for an inipi ceremony, and when those on the quest return parched, hungry, and weak, they undergo the final rounds. Those from the circle who are not on the quest take turns watching the fire every hour of day and night. I volunteered for a night—a beautiful and easy task. For an entire night I stayed awake to pray for those on the mountain, and for others.

Around midnight I sat peering into the fire. The fire's glow and warmth and my drowsiness transported me back to a September trip in the Sangre de Cristo Mountains. It looked like the last backpack of the season. Cold weather would be arriving soon along with the inevitable hunters and their guns, mechanical toys and noise. Don, Dick, Bill, Terrye, and I hiked three miles up a mountain canyon. The trailhead was 9,000 feet and we climbed to 10,500 feet, the trail following an old mining road that grew progressively rocky and narrow the farther that we hiked into the wilderness.

Like most late summer days, it had been very warm and dry. A few thunderheads rose east over the mountain crest, but we had not been affected on the drier west side. Night would be very cold, and aspens had begun turning to brilliant yellow with a small grove of bright orange here and there. The trip was a small pause in an otherwise hectic time of the year. Our drive to the trailhead was leisurely and not at all hurried, which meant that we caught up on each other's accomplishments over the past summer.

Hiking into the campsite was more like a stroll than a march. Although carrying enormous packs with lots of clothes, cool daytime temperatures kept us from overheating. We hiked along a vibrant, rolling creek, pure Rocky Mountain water splashing about in its many turns down the steep mountainside. Shaded by tall spruce and fir, the trail followed the canyon bottom while occasionally climbing up to the valley's south-facing side, where groves of aspen prospered in the brilliant sun.

A campsite was located at the intersection of three trails, two of which wound higher toward the mountain crest and elevations at 13,000 feet. We took the southern branch that ultimately reaches a high lake at over 12,000 feet, squatting below a peak well over 13,000 feet. Just past the intersection was a large grove of aspens that had grown up after a forest fire many decades ago. Our timing was perfect—the trees were nearing optimum color. In the cool, brilliant sunlight the scene was almost an illusion. It seemed surreal to have such bright yellows fluttering gently on the breeze. The light cast a golden glow down on the trail.

That night after dinner we stoked up the fire. The glow of the coals was entrancing. At peace and mellow with the realization that the snows would soon come to this beautiful land, I stepped back from the fire to glance up at the stars. Ten feet from the fire I felt a rain of minute ice crystals on my face. "Hey guys, it's snowing." Everyone stepped back. It wasn't snowing or raining, it was icing. A huge thunderhead far to the east was producing ice crystals that were being blown westward. The thunderhead must have towered at least forty thousand feet out over the high prairie to the east of the divide. The minute crystal gently floated down to the forest and our faces.

It was also quite cold standing back from the flames, and we returned quickly to regenerate our warmth. The glow of the fire lit the aspens with their golden aura. This was one of those special moments when the whole world and life seem just right and interconnected. Surrounded by friends, a sense of peace and calm enveloped our camp. The warmth of this beauty and fire had all of us nodding off.

I jerked noticeably and came out of my trance with a start. The late night had set in. "Oh yes, I'm watching the fire for others on the mountain." This was a difficult time as cool valley air overwhelmed the small fire. By 3:00 a.m. I was tired, cold, and thirsty. However, I was sacrificing so that my prayers for those on the mountain could be heard. I stoked the fire and decided that another log could wait. At precisely that moment I looked up and saw the most beautiful red meteor streak across the sky.

Later that morning when the shaman came to relieve me he asked if I had seen anything unusual. "It is amazing what you will see at night around this sacred lodge. Many strange things have been seen." I was startled at this revelation. "I saw a bright red meteor streak across the sky at low altitude." "Oh, really," was the shaman's reply. Later, a friend in the circle told me that the shaman interpreted this as some departed relative or friend traveling across the sky to greet me.

Inipi ceremonies, vision quests, and blessing ceremonies have helped me to understand better the Circle of Life and connectedness of all things here on Turtle Island—Mother Earth. Rocks used in inipi ceremonies represent departed grandmothers and grandfathers who are the wisest elders. They have the power to hear prayers, to provide guidance, to heal, to inform us of traditional ways, and to grant special requests. Are the emblems of the inipi ceremony really any different from other religious ceremonies? The central focus is a Supreme Being, God, Creator, and Great Spirit who lovingly attends to creation. It just so happens that the rituals and symbols in Native American spirituality also emphasize a person's relationship with nature. Nature represents the very manifestation of God.

The interconnectedness of all things as a central tenant of Native American spirituality fascinates. Yet how can so many profess humanism in our society? We are all in this together on the planet—every person and animal, all life, has a critical role to play. But humans continue to act as though they were superior to everything. How presumptuous. It is a fatal assumption that is leading civilization to a disastrous end and that is antithetical to a culture that deeply loves the earth. The ego of man is awesome to contemplate against the backdrop of a beautiful planet.

It is not necessary to traipse down to your local sweat lodge to get a sense of the sacredness of living in harmony with Mother Earth and the connectedness of all life. One of the easiest wake-up calls is to simply go outside at night and gaze on the wonder of the universe—an infinite creation that renders any one human's impact insignificant. Of course, those living in a city may have a difficult time seeing the sky and its stars because of light pollution. But virtually all of us can orchestrate a short journey to the country in seeking the stars. Away from light pollution, you are better able to understand that this magnificent planet is only one of an infinite number of worlds.

Several years ago a magazine published a startling photograph that should humble every inhabitant on this planet. The Hubble telescope was directed toward one of the seemingly empty parts of space. The resulting image was mind-boggling. There were galaxies, after galaxies, after galaxies as far as the Hubble telescope could see. Each galaxy contains billions of stars. The Hubble view was equivalent to focusing on a grain of sand held at the end of an extended fingertip.

Think of it, galaxies upon galaxies with billions of stars just by focusing at a point equivalent to a grain of sand. Now how important are you, or six billion people on earth? Certainly this is a unique and beautiful planet with an incredible capacity to support life. However, in the universal scheme of things we are certainly not the only game in the universe. We should reverently honor all that exists on this planet rather than presumptuously think that we are the center of the universe. That's little thinking by little people.

Annie Dillard quantifies the spectacular cosmos outside of spaceship earth and thus enables us to grasp the vast potential beyond our planet: "Ten years ago, I read that there were two galaxies for everyone alive. Lately, since we loosed the Hubble space telescope, we have revised our figures. There are maybe nine galaxies for each of us—eighty billion galaxies. Each galaxy harbors at least one hundred billion suns. In our galaxy, the Milky Way, there are four hundred billion suns—give or take 50 percent—or sixty-nine suns for each person alive." Try to think small again after rereading these figures and glancing up at the night sky.

Get out of your city; get out of your car to open yourself to this testament. I was driving a group back to San Diego from a collegiate academic contest in Reno, Nevada. Rather than stay another night, we decided to head home early. Little did I know that they all meant to sleep while I drove. Before losing elevation on the way to Bishop, California, on the eastern slope of the Sierra Nevada, we encountered several snow squalls. The road was treacherous and I was totally focused on our safety.

We exited a cloud of dazzling snowflakes lit up by the headlights, and I began to relax a bit. Suddenly our professor's voice came out from nowhere, "Pull over to the side of the road. Slow down and pull over." I did not question his authority. "What's the matter?" I whispered. He replied, "I just want to take a look at the sky. Keep the engine running. We won't be long." While the rest slept, we silently left the metal tomb to be challenged beyond comprehension. There in the crystal-clear Sierra Nevada night we were blessed with the cosmic glow. There was no moon. There were only stars upon billions of stars. Starlight would forever have new meaning.

Inipi ceremonies, vision quests, and blessing ceremonies have also helped me understand what it is like to be a minority and the connections to personal challenges. Although granted the privilege of sharing in these ceremonies, I am often the only non-Native involved. This experience has helped me to better comprehend in a very small way what minorities must feel, confront, and fight every day of their lives. My initial experience with the inipi ceremony represents what minority people go through when they tackle something new in dominant society. I simply did not know what to expect in the sweat lodge once I entered. This lack of knowing produced great anxiety—anxiety that made me put off participating in the first place. After I entered the lodge, my entire base of knowledge and experiences shouted for me to leave—too hot, too steamy, too enclosed. My coping mechanisms were thrown out the window.

The inipi has also taught me that I can never truly be an Indian. Unlike others who "wanna be" Indians, I simply desire to inculcate the best of some of their spiritual beliefs and practices. No matter how accurately I may mimic these customs and values, I do come from another tribe. I can still appreciate and treasure their gifts even though I am not one of them.

A late January inipi ceremony taught me this lesson very well. I arrived at the lodge late from work totally unprepared to partake but drawn to the lodge after a hard, stressful week at work. I parked my car along the country-like lane with overhanging trees accenting the natural setting of the lodge. Darkness was just overtaking the day. The air was rich with the smell of damp earth and decaying leaves intermingled with the unforgettable scent of a cedar fire. Nearing the lodge, a red glow of a very hot fire illuminated the night. "Mitakuye oyasin. Good evening." An initial prayer was offered to the glowing grandmothers and grandfathers. A gift of tobacco was shared with the fire in sending prayers to the Great Spirit.

Conversation before an inipi ceremony is low-key and measured by great periods of silence. I asked the shaman about the structure of the prayer altar and the significance of the emblems. He took the time to teach. In the meanwhile, a few men began to arrive. What had started as a group of four swelled to about ten. My thoughts about entering the lodge were vanishing. I listened carefully to ascertain who would be "pouring water"; that is, leading the ceremony. An appreciation had been developed for which shamans would bring a neophyte along through the four rounds of the ceremony, and which saw a challenge to turn the heat up.

Two friends suggested that they sit on each side to help me get through the ceremony. It sounded like a great idea, but the number of participants kept growing. Finally, the discussion indicated that an elder from Pine Ridge would be conducting the ceremony. That cemented it. I offered to pull rock for the benefit of all. We milled around for another hour adding a few logs to the fire until the shaman arrived. In his seventies, he meant for this sweat to be a cleansing one. Word passed discreetly among the crowd that this was a special sweat and there would be no leaving the lodge until all rounds were finished.

Several of the participants were preparing for a Sun Dance, and thus the ceremony was dedicated to showing support from other members in the circle. A very hot sweat would toughen the Sun Dancers and manifest the willingness of others in the circle to sacrifice for their brothers. The shaman called all to line up for entry into the lodge— on the order of fifteen people. Some were sitting at the very edge of the fire pit. They would have to contend not only with the intense heat, but also splatters of steam and scalding water when it was poured on the fire. The shaman said a few words of welcome and began a lesson followed by rituals. He called, "Bring in the rocks." Usually only a quarter of the rocks are brought into the lodge at each round.

I began pulling rocks and presenting them for placement by the shaman. There were more than sixty rocks in the fire. It is a very hot task to reach in with a pitchfork and sort the rocks from the red-hot coals, and then blow off ashes before presenting them to the lodge. I was sweating in absolutely no time. The hair on my arms was singed from the heat. I breathed heavily with so much work to complete in a very short time. I did not have time to think what it must be like in the packed lodge. I was the one taking all the heat right now, but it was gradually becoming overwhelming inside.

In the middle of this chore I glanced down at my shoes. Here I was in expensive slacks, a dress shirt, and $265 Allen-Edmonds dress shoes. I doubt that anyone has ever pulled rock dressed like this. Finally, the last rock was delivered. Standing off to the side of the open lodge, awaiting instructions for this emblem or that off the altar, I was overwhelmed by the heat coming out the door. What must it be like to be inside? By this point several inside were coughing and clearing their throats as their bodies tried to cope with this sudden immersion into the heavenly heat.

The shaman asked for the water to be brought in. I picked up the pail, offered some to the fire and the altar, and handed the pail through the door. He continued with his lesson and then told me to close the door. After doing so, I had a chance to stand up straight and stretch. Suddenly the air was cooler. I was a sweaty mess, but what must it be like in the lodge? I heard the sound of water being poured on the glowing rocks; prayers and chants ensued, and I began to pray for the well-being of those inside. This was a special time in tending the coals, heaping them into a neat pile, and turning thoughts to those in need.

A long chant finished, and the circle shouted, *"Mitakuye oyasin!"* This was my directive to open the door. A flood of hot steam came roaring out of the lodge. I cannot begin to fathom what the temperature must have been like inside. The release of energy and spirits was impressive. This elder was teaching the young ones a thing or two about humility and perseverance. I think the message was that this inipi would be like child's play compared to the challenge they would face at the Sun Dance.

The circle went through four rounds of praying. After the third round, one of the elder members of the circle thanked the shaman: "Grandfather, thank you for having mercy on us by opening the door." However, not a single person asked to leave. When they exited they were totally spent. As they emerged into the cool night air, their bodies gave off billows of steam. Each gave thanks to me for the power of my fire. I was the one who should give thanks for being part of a circle founded on a fundamental belief in the Great Spirit.

An inherent beauty of wildness is the pervasive interconnectedness of all living beings and their fit within the natural environment. Enlightened cultures, such as many from the Native American tradition, uplift both connections and nature. Human supremacy is seen as presumptuous and inconsistent with harmonious relations among all beings and the earth. Consequently, Native Americans ascribing to traditional ways are often offended by the dominant culture they encounter; a culture that promotes gratuitous materialism, disregard for the environment, and denigration of life.

On a horseback journey across the Southwest, Douglas Preston had the good fortune to visit with the Ramah band of Navajos. In the course of learning their story Preston discovered a sense of resignation about the cultural changes the Ramah Navajos endured. Having suffered through successive exploitation by the Spanish, Mormons, Mexicans, and Americans, the Ramah's attribute their cultural decline and that of the natural environment to these invaders: "The earth doesn't want to give us nourishment like it did back then. Back then the earth was happy, the sun was happy, everything was happy that all the Navajos were there, happy with these people being Navajos . . . the grass was real *big*, the water was *everywhere*. But then after the *Bilagaanas* (Anglos) showed up. The earth started going down and was pretty unhappy. . . . If they didn't come, the earth still would have been happy with us." At least for the Ramah band of Navajos there is a distinct causal link between the decline of the natural environment and cultural disintegration resulting from invasion.

Native Americans do not own a monopoly on the belief that everything is connected or that all of nature is to be revered. They simply have demonstrated greater consistency and pervasiveness in inculcating these values within their communities. A culture that loves the earth ultimately recognizes the preeminent value of wildness and nature. Such a culture would borrow deeply from Native American traditions about the connectedness of life without feeling compelled to mimic all other aspects of Native ways. In the final analysis, none of our cultures will survive unless they collectively embrace the earth and treat it in a dignified and holy manner, acknowledging fragile connections among living and nonliving alike.

11
Circumambulating the
Giant Strawberry

Beginning life as a fresh, sparkling mountain stream fed by a massive snow pack in the San Juan Mountains of Colorado, the Rio Grande slowly makes its way down to the high desert of New Mexico. Along the way, other perky streams and creeks splashing down from the airy peaks of the Sangre de Cristos join in a relentless push to the sea. Long before it arrives there, people drain off portions of the Rio Grande for their various purposes—irrigation, light manufacturing, and drinking water. The result is a river that hardly resembles its former self—a muddy concoction mimicking cement more than water.

It was not always this way. In fact, the Rio Grande has been tamed for only sixty years. After calamitous floods in the early 1940s, the Army Corps of Engineers, the Middle Rio Grande Conservancy District, and the Bureau of Reclamation established a series of dams and levees that put the Rio Grande in its place. For farms, towns, and pueblos along its course, control of a once mighty river quelled the threats of periodic flooding and encouraged development to flourish. Homes, transportation, and businesses would never again fear the wrath of broad floods that for a moment took back the land.

Sixty years later, what once seemed like a great idea for encouraging development now manifests significant problems. Without seasonal flooding, which left rich nutrients, regenerated the soil, and filled the aquifer, the bosque is gradually dying, and with it the tremendous stands of cottonwoods that symbolize this rare riparian habitat. Flooding provided a perfect medium for the fuzzy balls of cottonwood seeds blown about by spirited spring winds. Rich mud and high water levels presented a wholesome combination for incubation, and with this medium the forest of the bosque thrived. Consequently, wildlife proliferated within this delicate but robust profusion of greenery and water. This legacy is now decaying.

The death of the bosque is so highly illustrative of our inability to see that everything is connected. Spring runoff and heavy flooding delivered a fresh supply of water, debris, and soil that laid waiting for the gales of April and May. Scattered to the winds by venerable old cottonwoods that had seen many previous cycles of river flooding and recessions, seeds arrived on fertile new ground. Warmed in the rich soil, seeds sprouted. As they took root, saplings became browse for deer and other wildlife. Through luck of location, several of the saplings grew rapidly in the hot summer sun and were subsequently replenished in spring with the essentials for extraordinary growth.

Maturing trees provided shade for grasses at their base and limbs for nesting birds. Drawn to the high canopy, hawks patrolled the verdant grasslands seeking moles, prairie dogs, snakes, and other morsels. Native shrubs sprang up in the cooler microclimate of the forest, a stark contrast to the searing sage, sparse grassy plains, and dusty mesas rising up from the bosque. Bear, deer, and elk were drawn down from the surrounding mountains to feed on the lush garden along the river course. The beauty of this wildness exemplified natural connections among river, rock, sun, sand, flora, wind, and fauna.

When we think in small, human ways that focus on our needs as preeminent and all others as secondary, inevitably the connectedness of life is lost. A culture that deeply loves the earth understands and uplifts the idea of natural relationships and rhythms. It presupposes nothing about the superiority of humankind and attempts to fit human endeavor within a natural context—a milieu that possesses an ancient architecture and profoundly intelligent understanding about how things mesh in beautiful, harmonious, and functional ways.

"He's going in for surgery and may lose a kidney. I don't think I have any choice but to be there in case he needs one of mine." I shared this with my friend Jim when connecting about final planning for ten days of bliss. We were about to embark on the walk of our dreams—circumambulating the Wonderland Trail around Mount Rainier—when I received that fateful phone call from my father. With a family history of kidney stones, it never occurred to me that the dreaded curse would prevent me from taking a hundred-mile walk around the most beautiful mountain in the world.

Planning this trip for several months, Jim wanted to bring his father, Bill, who had just turned sixty, and who owned a small parcel of land close to Mount Rainier National Park. Another enthusiastic friend, Dennis, indicated that he would like to join in the festivities. Given Mount Rainier's legendary rainy weather, we would likely need plenty of enthusiasm. The only concern I harbored was Dennis's leg. On the very last ski run of the season at Crystal Mountain, he fell and managed to break it. Nonetheless, Dennis was determined to go once he heard about the trip, and to his credit he began a rigorous rehabilitation program to prepare for our hike.

A hundred-mile walk around a mountain offers many metaphorical reflections of life and interconnections. For one thing, in the course of a circumambulation, the beginning is also the end; we would walk a circle of life. For another, we would come to know Mount Rainier from all four sacred directions and thus catch a glimpse of the mountain as a whole. Finally, we would be exposed to all of Mount Rainier's climates from the sunny western slopes to the frigid north walls of ice and snow—glaciers with fantastic depth and imposing beauty. In the course of the walk we would see how forests on the sunny west side compare to the northeastern forests—fewer gigantic Douglas fir and hemlock, more raw exposure of stark rock and ridge, and more subalpine lakes, but fewer streams. In short, how the vegetation, water, and very topography of the land are connected—oriented—to the sun.

This circumambulation of Mount Rainier was also affected by other very evident connections. Family history threatened my ability to participate. Dennis's love for skiing the very snows that made Mount Rainier great, presented a significant personal challenge in his preparation and mileage that he could prudently walk. Preceding weeks of superb weather in the Pacific Northwest were inexorably linked with the cycles of sun, rain, and snow. In the end, we would learn indelible lessons about how everything is connected.

There are many times in life when you do not even have to think about a decision; there is really no other option. Such was the case when I received that phone call. My father would probably make it through surgery without any problems. However, this was just too risky. I needed to be there for him; I needed to be there for us. After checking the schedule for his operation and comparing it with our trip plans, I could still make the start of our hike if everything went just right. If not, then I would be joining the team in midstream. The surgeon indicated too much gravel in my father's kidney was causing infection that could be stopped only by removing the irritant. My dad went under the knife willingly, and the surgery was successful. But his recovery was problematic, and things became serious and scary.

Circumambulating the Giant Strawberry

I shared the bad news with Jim and Dennis that there would be no post-Labor Day start for me. It would be about three days before we would meet up. Jim said they would be camping down at North Mowich River on the west flank of Mount Rainier at that point. If I did not meet them then, I could catch them at the Carbon River. He recognized that I might not ever make it.

Dennis was relieved to hear about my plight. Not confident that his leg could take all one hundred miles of the trail with a pack, he would begin when I started and then end at the Sunrise Visitor Center, achieving approximately half the distance. We were off on a big adventure.

The Pacific Northwest had experienced an unusual period of warm, dry weather that August. Typically, the first and second weeks of August are free of rain and storms. July and late August are blemished by periodic storms lasting three days. In contrast, fall and spring are marked by five-day storms with few intervening dry periods. Winter is just one cloudy and wet mess—skies are literally gray for six months. The exception is generally the first week in January, when the sky clears to a brilliant blue. The temperature drops progressively into freezing range at sea level. Predictably, the next storm rolls in quite quickly and brings a foot of snow to the lowlands.

Our trip planning concluded when temperatures in the lowlands were constantly in the high eighty-degree range. There was no indication that this pattern would change in the next week or so, but count on dry, sunny weather in the Northwest and you are courting disaster. Add in the factor that we would be starting after Labor Day, and it was obvious that we would inevitably learn about what the Wonderland Trail looked like from beneath the hood of a rain jacket. Riding on optimism, I assembled my gear and provisions, trying to make the right connections with these weather cycles. From my father's bedside in San Diego, the necessity for raingear and insulation seemed unlikely. I concentrated on minimizing weight in order to make the circumambulation a reality.

Dennis picked me up at the house bright and early the day after I flew up from San Diego. With the crisis past for my father, he would be released within the next day. As I bid him goodbye, I was thankful for foregoing the initial start of our trip because now I could walk with peace of mind. Dennis and I scanned the map to determine the best starting point. Bill and Jim began at Longmire on the southern end of Mount Rainier, headed clockwise. Dennis and I would miss Indian Henry's Hunting Ground, St. Andrews Park, and Klapatche Park, but these were easily accessible on day trips or an overnight if I wanted to finish the loop. We would start our jaunt at the northern end of Klapatche Park off the end of the old Westside Road.

Getting there was half the fun because Dennis drove an old Mercedes sedan. We rode like kings. His wife would take the car back, and later pick Dennis up at Sunrise. Washington's weather could not be better. High temperatures were in the eighties at sea level and the seventies above. Only a few puffy clouds marred the horizon, but there was definitely no foreseeable change in the weather.

The Wonderland Trail intersects the Westside Road and North Puyallup River at 3,500 feet in elevation. We hoisted packs and began the long pull from the Puyallup Glacier up to Sunset Park and the Golden Lakes. Dennis had difficulty adjusting to his pack and the sudden reality that he would test his mending leg. Consequently, he set a slow pace heading through the forest north of the Puyallup Glacier, but we were free at last and embarked on the dream harbored during those rainy winter and spring days.

Most initial shakedowns are traumatic. Packs are at maximum weight and interfere with normal walking. It takes several miles and often days for things to smooth out. Dennis, of course, was having that much more difficulty, and he despised hiking through dense forest. On the other hand, I loved the tall Douglas firs and occasional stand of hemlock. Leaving a stream and glacial valley below, Northwest hikes tend to aim upward through two or three thousand feet of Douglas fir while the trees become progressively smaller. Dennis was bored at the scenery and irritated to find that his rehabilitation had not been as successful as he thought. But he continued to plug along at a pace of two miles per hour. As we learned, the routine was to climb up through forest to the four-thousand-foot level and progressive clearing. Rise steeply through the transition zone to subalpine country. Peak at a ridge and begin to head downhill immediately. In all, we estimated the elevation gain over the course of hiking one hundred miles on the Wonderland Trail to be around 32,000 feet.

I occasionally went ahead of Dennis as he fiddled with this part of his pack or delved into the cavern for a piece of food or clothing. The day was warm but not hot, and the slight breeze felt good as we began to exit the forest. Climbing up through the transition zone at 4,500 feet and what may have been the devastation of a fire, trees became scarce while the hillside was covered in low-growing shrubs and grasses of many varieties. Views opened up south to Mount Hood on the horizon, a symmetrical glaciated cone rising east of Portland, Oregon.

Despite the hot summer, the ridges to the south still wore their mantle of snow from the previous winter; they would soon receive a fresh coating of snow to begin the circle all over again. As for views of Mount Rainier itself, we had actually been too close to get a decent appraisal except for glimpses of the towering buttresses.

Climbing above five thousand feet, the trail headed north and west, and as we angled upward the mountaintop came into view. Here on the west side, lingering summer sun left great rock landscapes jutting up through snow and ice fields. Despite the progressive erosion of snow cover, the immense ice fields loomed above. Hundreds of feet thick, the icy blue glaciers of this volcano are awe-inspiring. They are also intimidating, since they exist on an active volcano that could come belching to life at any moment—witness Mount St. Helens, a mere sixty miles to the south as the crow flies. Public officials throughout the Puget Sound basin have awakened to the looming menace above them. Mount Rainier's glaciation would deliver a churning mass of water, mud, steam, and debris on a scale of magnitude that makes the Mount St. Helens eruption look like child's play.

The south end of Mount Rainier, Gibraltar Rock, was entirely free of snow and ice. The north end, Columbia Crest, was also somewhat free of ice and the impression of the mountain was a giant molar with ice in the middle. Down at six thousand feet, a great ridge flowing north and west from the crest, the Colonnade, was entirely free of snow and green with very low-lying shrubs and occasional stunted trees. The ridge itself was capped with rock detritus and the random patch of lingering snow. We could look down into the Puyallup River valley from which we had climbed and see the soft, thick stands of dark-green Douglas fir.

Out in the blazing sun, that forest looked enticing, even if Dennis thought it boring. Winding our way through the silvered trees, ghostly reminders of some violent past, we suddenly came upon a ptarmigan at the side of the trail. This grouse-like mottled brown and white bird was hunkered down in the foot-high shrubs. Its best defense was to remain stationary before foraging among berries and insects in this time of plenty and warmth. What extreme conditions it would be facing four months hence in the dead of winter with below-zero-degree winds from a storm blowing fresh billows of crystalline snow into drifts on this mountainside.

Eleven

The trail was beginning to level out and we intensified our searching for the Golden Lakes of Sunset Park. I thought we might catch up with Bill and Jim at this point because they were avid fishermen, but we were not worried about making contact. We had all essential cooking utensils and equipment between us; thus, it was entirely possible to walk to Sunrise without ever meeting them.

The trail climbed up into a swale of sheltered trees and we came upon a small group of people stopped on the edge of the trail. There, foraging among the downed relics of an ancient forest, was a large black bear. The bear was fifty yards away on a slight upslope, paying us no attention. Its coat was distinctive, with a light brown cape all across the back and that covered a jet-black head, black legs, and black undercarriage. I remembered seeing a similar effect among young folk who peroxide the top of their hair—so this is where the idea came from.

The trail wound to a patrol cabin set amid a pastiche of enticing lakes and tarns—about twenty bowls and three large oval-shaped lakes with water characteristic of the typical Northwest subalpine lake—that is, a very deep blue-emerald green. Bright sun illuminated the clarity of this refreshing water while a slight breeze dimpled the surface. These were high mountain lakes that only warmed up at the end of the season—there was just a hint of foreboding in the face of these waters. They certainly knew what arctic conditions would be like in this subalpine basin.

At the Golden Lakes patrol cabin, a hiker sat on the porch eating lunch. We exchanged greetings as we passed. I caught a glimpse into the dark cavern of the cabin. It looked cold and dismal, but I bet that impression could change fast in a strong, steady rain in the lower forty degrees. Under those conditions, the cabin would look very inviting given the expansive exposure of Sunset Park. We were now at 5,000 feet on the ridge curving above the largest of the Golden Lakes whose basin was down at 4,600 feet. We did not need to replenish our water, which was everywhere. We eased down the trail into a growing collection of trees and began the 2,500-foot descent to the Mowich River.

Most people would agree that there is nothing as beautiful as a warm, but not hot, cloudless and windless day in the Northwest above timberline. Everything just shimmers with life and light. You have been blessed with an extraordinary day, and you savor its blessings, but it all seems just a little bit overwhelming, almost fake. It will eventually end, if not tomorrow, the day after. Accustomed to experiencing mountains under less than perfect conditions, that perfection takes on a patina of falsehood. This cannot be real; it is just too beautiful. Additionally, there is the realization that it will spoil what you have come to appreciate as good days—days when it was only misting instead of raining; days when the stiff breeze added an edge to a cloudless sky; days when warm overcast and the subdued grays were perfectly acceptable; and days when you felt good just to get out. A perfect Northwest day only increases your hunger for more, and you know that what had been acceptable can no longer meet the test.

In retrospect, Dennis and I should have been overjoyed in the soft, silent, cool forest into which we dropped. The trail was cushioned by plenty of needles fallen over decades. The forest was still and embracing, not dark and foreboding. It made the miles pass easily until we could see down into the South Mowich River, frothing with water from melted ice from high up the mountainside.

At three thousand feet the trail began to level a bit, and we looked forward expectantly toward camp for the night. We became concerned about our ability to cross the milk-white river, clanging with the sound of boulders being driven down the valley by the rushing torrent. Our apprehension grew as the trail began to leave the forest for the alluvial plain. The river bottom was littered with small boulders that were obtrusive to walking and unpleasant after many miles of soft tread in the forest. Just when our apprehension rose to a fever pitch, there was the way across the braided torrent. The Park Service had erected two logs across the most challenging channels. These logs were anchored with cables, but they definitely would not be around next spring.

We paused on the logs to look up over the rocky till left by the Puyallup Glacier toward the fields of ice, now high above us. I thought briefly about the phenomenon of ice dams—meltwater blocked by ice that suddenly flushes past the dam and creates a torrent of flood proportions. This was certainly a great time for this to occur at the end of a warm day, but the gods spared us. In a few minutes all of the travail was behind, and we entered forest above the river bottom winding through stands of willow and alder. What a stark contrast to the river bottom—overwhelming life arising from the rock, silt, and water only dozens of feet below. I parted a few willow branches blocking the trail and then was suddenly confronted by a large gnome in shorts and a bright red vest. It was Jim.

Bill and Jim were picking salmon berries for dessert, and they waded through the five-foot-high shrubs collecting all that they could find.

Bill had a nice plateful, offering a contrasting color relief to the dominantly green glen—green moss, green trees, green shrubs. How could there possibly be so many shades of green? Jim indicated that he had considerable luck in catching fish up at Golden Lakes, and they were supplementing dinner with their catch. That was good, because Jim was never known for gourmet meals out on the trail. His philosophy seemed to be just bulk up and wait until civilization for the finer aspects of cuisine. That's probably the way things should be. Focus on being there, rather than the technology of being there.

They had a nice little campfire going. A "nice little campfire" in Pacific Northwest terms is essentially a smoldering pile of wet wood, and this was a classic fire with few flames and plenty of dense smoke. Just the same, it added a touch of the cook fire to the setting, and we began to feel at home. I selected a campsite and checked it for its draining properties. The tent went up easily enough, but at the last moment I pondered about the rain fly. It had been a fabulous day, and the forecast was for continuing fine weather. However, it is always easier to set up a rain fly in daylight rather than in the rainy dark. Reacting to a vast experience of wet weather, I added the fly and we got down to the business of cooking dinner.

For dinner I brought macaroni and cheese with meat additive. It sounds lousy right now, but go hike a dozen or more miles with a pack on and you will begin to see the beauty of such a meal. It fills you up and provides calories that you crave even if it lacks taste. Trout and berries— delicious in a rugged, camping sort of way—accentuated the macaroni.

I took the dirty dishes over to rinse them off at the stream and Jim tagged along. He confided, "I didn't think my father was going to make it." "Is he all right now?" I asked. Jim went on to explain, "He was very, very slow the first two days on the trail. He was not breathing well and moved as slowly as a slug. I thought we would have to turn back before Indian Henry's Hunting Ground. I worried about him having a heart attack. However, today was a very good day. I think he is adjusting to the rigors of the trail." "Do you think we should pull out at Carbon River?" I asked Jim. "Nope, if we just go slowly and carefully I think he will be okay. One day at a time." We finished cleaning the dishes and headed back to camp. Shortly after dark and the warm camaraderie of the campfire, we retired to bed.

And the next morning? You bet—rain. We came out of our tents in disbelief. How could it be raining? The weather had been so perfect.

We were disappointed. Having slogged through years of Northwest weather, it would be lying to say that rain brought a new perspective to the land after several weeks of dry, warm weather. We knew rain. We knew how to get about in rain. We knew to keep going even though it was raining. However, a rainy morning just made our hearts ache after all of those previous beautiful days.

Hurrying through breakfast, I had my usual hot oatmeal and hot chocolate. We picked up the soggy tent and drenched rain fly, secured sleeping bags in plastic bags, and headed up the trail. Up, because there are only two directions on the Wonderland Trail—down or up. This morning would be up from 3,000 feet to Spray Park at 6,300 feet before dropping to the Carbon River, again at 3,000 feet.

Wearing gray shorts with a white cotton T-shirt, I put on my rain parka and synthetic cap. Jim and Dennis also donned their shorts, while Bill continued on in his long pants. We proceeded to swing northeast and then east as we gradually gained elevation above the North Mowich River and Eagle Cliff. The forest was dense, composed of thick Douglas fir and hemlock. With one long switchback after another, and given the mist, fog, and trees, there was very little to focus on other than Dennis's boots. We finally stopped for a snack break at Lee Creek at a little under five thousand feet. Rich vegetation, including cow parsnip, yarrow, and columbine, dominated the creek side—a lush meadow with a happy, splashing stream about three feet wide. The Park Service provided a slippery footbridge across the creek, but it was unnecessary, and in the wet conditions more dangerous than none. Surrounding trees were becoming smaller in size and topping out at about thirty feet. I could sense the beginning of subalpine country.

As we entered Spray Park, the clouds lifted slightly and provided a view toward Russell Glacier. This was high and lonesome country that probably did not see much in the way of foot traffic beyond the Wonderland Trail and a few climbers who tired of the popular routes. Stopping for lunch just as the clouds came back down, we were enveloped in mist. The penetrating cold cut lunch short. Our rain parkas came back out and we were ready to set off. However, Dennis was lingering and felt the need to rest. He had a habit of taking long lunch breaks and was not about to violate this habit despite the mist. We waited for a while out of courtesy and then, impatient, set off when the chill became too much. Far better to be hiking tired and warm than rested and cold. The trail narrowed to a foot-deep rut through the heather, whose bright pink blossoms provided some cheer on an otherwise dismal walk.

Within ten minutes we came to a perpetual snowfield cum glacier at Spray Park. The trail headed directly across the snowfield. Although it had been used all summer, the trail was indistinct in the fog and mist enveloping us. In fact, it was downright invisible. I worried about Dennis's ability to find his way in the gathering darkness, even though it was only three o'clock in the afternoon. Ahead we saw a six-foot-tall rock cairn proclaiming the way. I stopped and looked behind only to see the mists rise for a brief second. There was Dennis hoofing it as fast as he could go. We shouted to him just as the mists began to descend and we gathered together in safety, chattering to relieve the sense of anxiety from uncertainty about the trail and Dennis's ability to find the way. He realized that it might be difficult finding the route given the weather, and after we departed he had had second thoughts. However, we were setting too fast a pace for him to catch up and he feared he would be lost in the swirling mist.

The rock cairn marked the apex of Spray Park. We would drop a couple of hundred feet in making our way through Seattle Park and picking up Marmot Creek on our way down to Cataract Creek. It must be lovely country, perhaps even better than Golden Lakes, judging by the amount of water and ice in the area. I will have to go back there some early August day to see what I missed. As for the group, we knew what lay ahead—downhill.

The trail dropped very steeply with horrible erosion in spots. We were flying now trying to keep warm and ready to reach our next camp. Below the five-thousand-foot level the trees began to spring up again amid the rocks, and it seemed only a matter of minutes before the way plunged down through the forest and a campsite near Cataract Falls. The campsite was already occupied, and it looked like a muddy, wet mess. A group at the site had clear plastic tarps spread overhead, but this looked like a dismal place to share camp. On we went in the rain down toward the Carbon River.

That night we set up camp off trail in a gully with hemlock and fir. We just hoped that it did not rain any more; otherwise, we would be floating in our own pool next morning. Since we were not in an official campsite, we did not have a fire. I wonder whether we could have found any dry wood had we decided to try one. As usual, I took responsibility for hanging out food. A bear has never accosted us, but we certainly did not want to have the experience now. We ate dinner quickly and went to bed in an effort to keep everything dry. Our years of hiking in the rain told us that you keep critical gear dry. Once something gets wet, it is near impossible to dry it out as long as the moisture continues to fall. With the deep duff of the fir and hemlock, my half-inch Ensolite foam pad was comfortable enough. We had earned a good rest, and it did not take long before we all were deep asleep.

Cold the next morning, we deliberated about terminating the hike, given convenient access to the Carbon River Ranger Station. This was a difficult decision, inasmuch as Jim and his father were now halfway around the mountain. To add confusion, the sun came bursting forth and shed a new light on the land. Steam began to rise from logs, rocks, and anything else that captured the warming rays. Clouds in our minds lifted and sun chased away pessimism, so we immediately finished packing. By now the tent was a soaking mess of water and had gained substantial weight. The good news was our rations were lower and walking was fun once again. However, as we stood at the cut bank just below Cataract Creek, we tried to determine where the trail crossed the roaring maelstrom of the Carbon River. Steam continued to rise in zephyrs as sun warmed the grounds and plants. Jim came back from a short foray upstream and said that a bridge was ahead. We were underway.

All of the excitement returned with the sun, the bridge, the glacier, and the prospects of a bright and new day. First we had to negotiate the bridge. It was more like a narrow plank strung high above the milk-white froth of the raging Carbon River. The Carbon Glacier is one of the major ice masses on Mount Rainier, and the Carbon River confirmed this fact. We could not have forded this river without the bridge. The crack and growl of boulders being swept along in the wild currents warned of dangerous currents. Presumably, this impressive torrent grew in volume and strength as the day wore on. I hopped up to be the first to cross, and only then did the nervousness set in. You had to step up about three feet on rock steps to the narrow footpath down the middle of the bridge with little more than about one foot in width to negotiate. At waist level were two steel cables that spanned the river and served as grips when crossing the river. This was not nice.

The last thing you wanted to do was to look down into the churning blender of river. It would hurt to fall off this bridge and your entry into the river would present a distinct challenge for survival. That water had to be near freezing, having just exited from the Carbon

Glacier. It seemed like an eternity, but I was soon working my way up the final ten feet on the eastern bank. I turned in relief to watch the others cross and to give them encouragement. No one had any problems. Even Dennis was able to move along pretty well despite his past injury. With that chore over, we turned to the glacier ahead. The snout was dark gray ice with a cap of soot-black rock. The front face was very jagged and about 150 feet high. Out of the west center of this face flowed the source of the Carbon River. It was splashing and churning at abandon. In front of the ice were vast piles of rock debris left from the glacier's retreat in these warmer times.

The entire atmosphere was charged with crackling from ice breaking apart. Occasionally the glacier emitted a groan and the sound of falling rock was persistent as small to large boulders finally left their host. These rocks were the very mountain. Carried from the ice and rock gardens above, they had made the trip several miles down to the lowland only to be ultimately dumped as a debris field. This was a living, breathing, moving mass, and it was quite unstable.

Soft powder-blue skies continued to show breaks in the clouds and occasional showers of sun down on the glacier. After we walked for half a mile along glacial till, the Wonderland Trail began to switchback above the massive glacier. With many steep turns, the trail climbed dramatically upward. This was no gentle grade. Part of the problem was getting above the glacier while also finding a way through the rocky crags that squeezed the glacier at this point. The glacier's chill had its impact on these rock faces, for the vegetation was unique to this point on the trail. Dense Alaskan cedars grew from rocky perches and shared their beautiful green foliage, much like small sequoias.

The way was tough but enchanting as we climbed steadily. Lost in a world of exertion, I did not notice that we were now gaining substantial elevation and reaching tree line. Coming over a rise, we ran into another group camped at the side of the trail. The sun's rays were warming their camp, and they were out with their sleeping bags trying to remove a bit of moisture. This was a lovely rock garden with a profusion of wildflowers and greenery spread throughout the area.

Lazy marmots waddled around on the rocks. They, too, were ready for sun that they had once taken for granted over the last three weeks. Their thick brown coats glistened in the sun as they spread languorously, fat and sassy, peering at us through beady eyes over their rock thrones. Much scurrying ensued if we came too close. Their brethren the pikas were also running about with great purpose and industry. High-pitched squeaks sounded alarms over imaginary invasions by the group of humans lumbering past. What good cheer they added to the day. But were we any different, with our measured stride and serious travel bound for a distant site? They enjoyed their day in the sun and we ours.

I looked up from their rock piles to the towering cliffs shrouded in mists above. Above were the Elysian fields, an enticing cirque of tarns, ponds, and mini-lakes just west of Vernal Park. I would like to know those fields some day.

Our mood was much more jovial as the trail began to flatten out. Snow banks remained in this high country and the trail was just beginning to resurface. In a few more weeks the process would reverse itself. In spots, water gently cascaded down the trail. Marsh marigolds were prolific in this wet and wonderful world.

We could now begin to catch sight of Willis Wall, the fabled north face of Mount Rainier. What a sight it was. Heavy glaciations on the north face were not affected by warm summer days—it was all snow and ice in disarray. Willis Wall, a sheer rock face, was more ice than mineral. Dropping off Liberty Cap was a glacial forked tongue, Carbon Glacier to the west and Winthrop Glacier to the east. They presented as powerful a statement about heavy precipitation as could be made in the lower forty-eight states. Two major rivers—the Carbon River and White River—owe their existence to these massive ice fields. This was the Pacific Northwest at its finest.

I stopped for a snack and looked back. The trail was a dirt path, not deeply rutted, but winding through the rocks, trees, and rivulets. Subalpine flowers with their delicate colors abounded in profusion including the ubiquitous marsh marigold, pasque flower, glacier lilies, and columbine. Fir and spruce showed the ravages of a high, wet, and cold country. Skinny and misshapen, some were still bent under the weight of snow.

Vistas continued to open to the south toward the mountain as we entered Moraine Park, a roughly half-mile-long bench of beauty. It was an incredible backdrop, with Willis Wall towering above, yielding a decidedly surreal sensation. Here we were in subalpine/alpine conditions that contrasted significantly with the lowland rainforest we had left behind only a couple of hours earlier. In the chilled air by a couple of tarns at eight thousand feet below the sheer face of Willis Wall and

Eleven

Liberty Cap, we had traveled from one world into another and stood there dwarfed by the next. It was a powerful, humbling feeling.

A cloud cap dominated the summit and gray skies loomed to the west as we began the descent to Mystic Lake, our home for the night. Dropping down half a mile and about five hundred feet of elevation to the lake, we remained in sunny subalpine country. Out came all the gear in an effort to dry things in the occasional sun and a time of replenishment. Jim went off to fish and the rest of us moseyed about the camp taking care of this concern or that. The temperature was falling, and the difference from the temperate humidity of the previous camp was all too apparent. Nature's refrigerator loomed above us, and sudden downdrafts of cold air came sweeping across camp.

On finishing supper I began to look for a place to hang our food. Spruce trees between Jim and Bill's tent were no more than twenty feet high and about six inches in diameter. There etched into the trees on either side of their tent at about eight feet were deep incisive claw marks from a bear. Apparently someone else had hung a cache overnight between the two trees, only to have a hungry visitor try to join in on the offering. I looked with renewed vigor about one-quarter of a mile down the trail and returned to my formerly substantially dry tent in a light rainsquall. I was now back to where I had begun the day.

The next day dawned cold, wet, and windy, so we hurried through a perfunctory breakfast and hit the trail. Clouds and mist obscured the mountain and we walked on in quiet silence. A big challenge ahead was crossing over the White River at the snout of Winthrop Glacier, but by this point our confidence was very high. There was very little that we could not tackle. Bill had gotten into shape. Dennis and his leg had come to terms. The task for the day was clearly defined. We merely had to slog through wind and rain to reach Sunrise.

It was a day without much social sharing. Forest on each side of Winthrop Glacier's trough held stunted trees that had poor soil for growth. Crossing the White River turned out to be a nonevent because we were so close to the glacier and it was so early in the morning that the water level was quite low. Additionally, instead of just one major crossing, there were several branches there in the alluvial plain. Spindly logs had been placed across each crossing. We could only speculate on what a challenge this must be early in the season.

Dense stands of fir kept the effects of the wind at bay until we were climbing the last eight hundred feet into Berkeley Park. By this point we all were wearing complete rain and wind gear with our hoods up. Wind was roaring across the barren landscape and I began, for the first time, to wonder if I carried sufficient clothing to cope with the gales. This dilemma was becoming serious since the wind had a deep frosty bite to it. Just when I thought I would have to use my last source of heat we topped a ridge and I could see the outbuildings of Sunrise. This had not been a fun day, and the monotony of walking in rain, cold, and wind was taking a toll on our spirits. I wasn't here just to put a pack on and move it ten miles down the trail. I wanted to have fun. Except for the brief respite at Moraine Park, the last three days had begun to lose their meaning. Fun was a bygone thought left in the sunny ramparts of the Golden Lakes.

Down in the soggy campground, I put on a wool shirt but was still cold. Dennis asked why I did not put something else on to warm up and I replied, "This is all I brought. The weather had been so nice that I didn't think I would need anything else." In return he offered, "Well, I guess you can borrow this light pullover sweater. It should keep you from freezing to death." Freezing to death. I had not thought of that.

Jim and Bill commenced to set up their tent just as the rain turned to snow. Dennis left for Sunrise Lodge and his wife. I sort of milled around. Freezing to death. I certainly did not factor that in and now it was snowing a goodly amount. Freezing to death. Hmm. Then something clicked in my head.

This is stupid. I did not sign up for snow or "freezing to death." Perhaps it's time to bail out? I did not have the equipment necessary to make it farther in these conditions, so I talked the matter over with Jim and Bill. They would wait until morning to leave if the snow did not let up. Deciding to go back with Dennis, I proceeded to run the half-mile or so to Sunrise Lodge. But by now there was no sign of Dennis, and I had psychologically committed myself to leaving. "This is crazy," I thought. "I did not bring a down coat or long underwear. I don't have my gloves or wool cap. I know how fast the snow can pile up around here." Dejectedly, I went out the lodge door, not very clear in my thinking. I wanted to leave now, not tomorrow.

In hindsight I should have stayed the night because in the morning I still could bail out just as easily as I could now. A young couple exited the lodge. "Are you going to Seattle?" I asked. "We were not planning on it till tomorrow. What do you need?" they said. Then it came gushing out about the rain, the wind, the rain, and snow. "Well, I guess we could leave tonight." I ran back to Jim and Bill to collect my pack. Just like that, the hike was over.

In the backseat of a Volkswagen van, it was great to be warm and dry, but weird to see the mountain slipping away at such fast speed. We drove down to the White River Entrance Station and out of the park. No sooner were we five miles from the White River entrance than clouds cleared and the sun came out. For the entire way to Seattle we enjoyed sunny weather, and I now know better. As a storm exits it is followed by cooler, dry air. Snow was simply a manifestation of dry air following the last dollop of precipitation.

I knew I had blown it, but in my mind I also knew that I was not properly equipped for the remainder of the trip, even with Dennis's sweater. What if the weather turned again when we were in the distant wilderness? Without the right equipment I would be in big trouble, not the least of which is a good probability of actually freezing to death.

Watching sunny weather in Seattle convinced me that I had erred seriously in my decision. High pressure dominated the Pacific Northwest and prospects were for another week of higher than normal tempera-tures. I decided to go back and intersect Jim and Bill, reasoning that they would have dropped down from Sunrise to the White River and back up to Summerland (a misnomer if I ever heard one). They would then camp at Indian Bar. I could drive to Ohanapecosh and take the three-mile Olallie Creek Trail up to the Wonderland Trail and hike north until I ran into them.

This time I packed long underwear, down parka, heavy wool cap, gloves, and mid-weight wool shirt. I knew that this equipment was nec-essary if the weather turned again, even if it meant that I had to carry a lot more weight. Early the next morning I left for Ohanapecosh, parked by the ranger cabin, and followed the trail up past Silver Falls to Olallie Creek.

Ohanapecosh has some of the most beautiful water in the world—crystal-clear and ambling along unlike the torrents found throughout the rest of the park—such as Laughingwater Creek, a mellow stream with a mesmerizing cobblestone bed and quiet waters.

The trail up Olallie Creek was a classic Pacific Northwest hike with huge Douglas fir down low and thick vegetation whenever the forest thinned. Judging by the overgrowth and tread of the trail, few people took this route. Entering portions of the trail where salal and devils club are six feet high or more, it became downright spooky. A crashing departure of some large mammal sent shivers down my spine—I could only think of the claw marks on the tree back at Mystic Lake.

Before long trees began thinning and getting smaller. I knew I was approaching the ridge on which the Wonderland Trail ran south from Ohanapecosh Park and Indian Bar. I reached a small saddle just above 4,500 feet amid twenty-foot-high trees, and the weather was picture perfect. I did not think that Bill and Jim could have gone down the mile to their next camp—Nickel Creek—but I checked the trail and found no evidence of recent boot tracks. The only option appeared clear—hike up the Wonderland Trail toward Indian Bar. With the gift of great weather, I started slowly up the trail. Cowlitz Divide presented expansive views toward the east side of Mount Rainier. Little Tahoma, an eleven-thousand-foot peak, loomed overhead. The beauty was not in the many glaciers—Ohanapecosh, Frying Pan, Whitman, Cowlitz, or Ingraham—but in the grassy subalpine parks with scattered clumps of trees. This was meadow country at its finest.

I would walk along for a while and then set down my pack and just gaze at this kinder, gentler side of Mount Rainier. Just two days earlier it had been snowing on these parks. Off in the distance Mount Adams was clearly visible as well as the Goat Rocks, a renowned area of saw-tooth peaks. To the south was Mount St. Helens and Mount Hood. I was in mountaineering heaven, given the warm sunshine and immersion in meadows. Continuing to make my way along the trail, I stopped occasionally to enjoy this panorama. I continued to scan the ridge ahead where it climbed up one thousand feet toward Ohanapecosh Park. I could see a couple of people coming down the trail and I convinced myself that it was Bill and Jim.

Rather than break the spell, I just waited in the lovely meadows. This must have been some flower garden a few weeks earlier. Now the flowers were past their prime and just the plants themselves remained. I could have made good use of a pair of binoculars to spot mountain goats and other game. I waited patiently while the figures of Jim and Bill began to increase in size. They came around the bend and were startled to see me waiting for them. "Hey, great to see you," shouted Jim. "Welcome back," grinned Bill. Without breaking stride, they swept past and I threw on my pack to keep up. They were definitely ready to be off this trail. I fell into step with them.

"How was the weather after I left?"

Eleven

"It snowed about three inches and was gone in the morning. I took a great shot of alpenglow on Mount Rainier that next morning. It was like a giant strawberry."

"Esther says hi. She sent along a few goodies for dinner."

"You missed a fantastic camp at Summerland. It was probably the most beautiful spot on the whole trip. Just above the camp you have to cross Panhandle Gap by the Sargent Glacier. It was very difficult crossing on the ice so early in the morning. But the view from the gap is out of this world."

"Maybe I will try it on the way back. How far is it to Summerland from the road?"

"We estimated about five miles from the campground. The trail is real easy and only switchbacks the last half mile."

And so the conversation went as we dropped down Cowlitz Divide toward Nickel Creek, where we set up camp and I pulled out fresh tomatoes and jams that Esther had sent along. These boys were ready for fresh food. Later that night after dinner, a chill came to the camp. The season was changing and I was extremely glad for my down coat. It was not cold, but I could feel the temperature drop after the sun went down, and I knew the balmy nights of two weeks ago were gone forever.

Morning arrived crisp and cool—no campfire this morning, for Jim and Bill were on a mission. There was very little talk as gear was stowed and packs hefted. They intended to hike seventeen miles to Longmire in one day. Bill took the lead and we were off. The trail parallels Stevens Creek from Nickel Creek two thousand feet up to Louise Lake and Reflection Lakes. Unfortunately, the park road also parallels Stevens Creek. We were in constant sight and sound of cars for the better part of the morning, but there was no stopping now. It was a nonstop pull from Nickel Creek all the way up to Louise Lake. We paused at Reflection Lakes to have a brief bit of lunch, where the wind came up and skies turned cloudy, but sun returned within the hour. In the next three hours we would pass several waterfalls that were anticlimactic after all the other beauty. The trail down from the lakes was uneventful, and in the middle of the afternoon the ranger station at Longmire came into view. The hike was over.

Bill and Jim were elated. It was a great accomplishment for them. By the end of the trip, Bill could hike like a person many decades younger. It was an amazing transformation. We loaded up Jim's car and they shuttled me over to Ohanapecosh, where I spent the evening at the car campground since I intended to visit Summerland the next day. It was very strange setting up a small backpacking tent amid the trailers, but I made do with my accommodations despite feeling insignificant.

Per custom, I awoke very early, ate breakfast, and drove over Cayuse Pass to the White River Ranger Station. It was another perfect morning. How long could this last? Parking at the bridge on Fryingpan Creek, there were only two other cars on the side of the road. Within an eighth of a mile I blew by a pair of hikers. "Wow, where are you going in such a hurry?" one of them asked. I had to explain that I had been backpacking for a week and without the pack I felt like I could fly. It was like a casual walk in fast forward.

The first three miles were a stroll through tall timber and the sound of Fryingpan Creek reminded me that the happy stream was constantly nearby. At three miles the trail broke free from the forest and entered a glacial valley hewn by ice. The trail crossed the creek, which was only mildly milky from glacial silt. A most notable geographic feature was the devastation wrought by massive avalanches from high on the glaciers. This would be a very dangerous place in winter. Across the creek the trail climbed another five hundred feet before coming to the beautiful campsites of Summerland. What a magical land it was.

To the north lay Goat Mountain. I could see a distant phalanx of white goats high in the meadows across the valley grazing slowly along in the warmth of the day. To the west were the Fryingpan Glacier and the nine-thousand-foot vertical rise of Mount Rainier. I could see why Jim was so impressed and reminded myself that the beauty of hiking the Wonderland Trail is our ability to see the mountain from different perspectives. There are so many beautiful ways to look at it. Sitting there amid the late summer flowers, I turned to the south and saw Panhandle Gap. After watching the marmots play for awhile, I decided that I had better get up to the Gap since it was still midmorning and I needed to reach the car soon, for I had no food with me.

The trail climbed over a snow cave hollowed out by a stream. This was dangerous business, since a fall through the snow would put me in a very difficult position in freezing water with no way out. I hurried along over the snow bridge and followed the barely discernible trail rising up across the ice. This was really getting treacherous. The next thing I knew, there I was halfway up this permanent snowfield with the footing deteriorating all of the time. I pressed onward and to the Gap. "Yes, this is a great view," I said to myself. Of course, having hiked up and down Cowlitz Divide, I had seen most of it anyway, so I turned to climb down.

"Okay. Focus on what you are doing. Gad, this is slippery." Anxiety began to set in. I walked up this mini-glacier; surely I could go down it. But there is that little fact of physical science that you have more traction going up rather than down. I made it to the middle of the glacier. That's when I made the fatal mistake of looking down. It swooped down and to the right. If I fell, I would slide quickly down onto the rocks. For more than a moment I was paralyzed. "Where is my ice ax now that I need it?" I asked myself. I was near panic—alone on the middle of a glacier in big trouble. Had I waited until later in the day, the ice would have melted a bit to make things easier. I sent up a prayer for safety. "Focus." "One step at a time." This was the equation that helped me out of one of the most dangerous moments of my life. Time passed oh so slowly and I was drenched in sweat despite standing there on a glacier. And then it was over. I was off and walking back down the trail.

Time to get home. Time to immerse myself in something other than Mount Rainier. I had tested the mountain one too many times, and the next faux pas could be my last. After racing down the trail with blinding speed, I jumped into the car and headed for Seattle. As I drove out of the park, the first high cirrus clouds formed overhead. The next day it would be raining and fall had officially replaced summer for good at Mount Rainier.

A long walk around a mountain brings many pleasures and pains in the course of the journey. However, there is a special reward in ending at the beginning. Our circumambulation of Mount Rainier was instrumental in understanding the many faces of a mountain—its microclimates, shady deep recesses, frolicking streams, icy cold glaciers, mellow meadows, sunlit western slopes, towering Douglas fir forests, rocky alluvial plains, and weather vagaries. This trip accentuated the connectivity of it all. By circling the mountain, we saw and experienced how it all fit together.

We learned significant lessons about the cycles and connectivity of weather—how a long warm spell in late summer will end without warning; how the tail end of storms ushers in colder temperatures and precipitation changes; how a slight chill in the morning air signals a shift in balance from one season to the next; and how glaciers sit waiting patiently for the next infusion of ice, coming in the clouds beyond the horizon.

Circumambulating Mount Rainier provided many perspectives on the circles of daily life and our connections with the land. In planning the trip, we conceptualized the trail as a walk between a series of points with topographical challenges thrown in. Our metric was the number of miles to be covered each day. Once on the trail we reframed our conceptual map to recognize the methodical climbs out of river valleys, up to subalpine ridges, and back down to the rough scars of rivers borne high on the mountain's glaciated slopes. Our new metrics were both miles and elevation, with the latter having a more significant connection to our task.

When the weather changed, significant connections with our daily routine became apparent. Attention focused on staying warm and dry while still negotiating the miles of trail, physical obstacles, and mental challenges. Camp routine remained the same, but with greater urgency and alacrity for getting the job done without compromising the veil of protection in dryness of tent, clothes, and sleeping bags. But, even more significantly, we began to understand how each day would unfold from rapid start in breaking camp, eating a hurried breakfast, and carefully packing equipment as a measure of protection for critical clothing; to the long slogs with head bowed into the wind and rain with intermittent short breaks to consume this morsel or that while briefly remarking on a natural phenomenon or scene of touching beauty; and finally to the glory of setting down the stone on our backs to reestablish a meager home there in the wilderness.

In many respects, our circumambulation of Mount Rainier became a metaphor for the interconnectivity of life. We came away understanding with greater clarity and insight that everything is connected. And, in the process, we learned that it is nature and wildness that ultimately rule—not us. We had to reframe our thinking about nature. The mountain did not.

As New Mexico has learned in attempting to control the Rio Grande, natural forces are vastly complex. Interconnections exist within nature that we do not understand, or worse yet, understand only partially. As a result, we often do more harm than good. Alan Watts captured the root of the problem in *Cloud-Hidden, Whereabouts Unknown*: "But man is making a mess of the earth because he is using his Euclidean intellect instead of his organic brain. He is symbolizing and describing nature along the straight or by the curve of the simplistic circle, and though such mathematicians as topologists and matrix theorists are capable of much more sophisticated operations, the averagely Western person still figures the world according to Euclid and to the arithmetic of decimation."

In this time of ecological crisis we are therefore into a big fight. A grand river and its bosque woodlands, or a great mountain with its glaciers, rivers and forests, deserve better thinking on our part. The mountains, seashores, prairies, canyons, river deltas, deserts, swamps, meadows, forests, and other ecosystems of this beautiful world offer a great reservoir of treasures. They provide opportunities for adventure and education to each of us if we simply open ourselves to their magic. They provide a milieu in which we can restore our balance with nature and ourselves. They are filled with life that persistently reminds us of our connections to each other. They reaffirm spirituality for those open to and seeking moments when they can be one with the world. These treasures remain hidden to those who see nature and wildness as something to exploit or control. In the end, each of us has a deep, personal responsibility to honor and uphold the gift of wildness and to contribute to a culture that loves the earth.

Sources

1. La Querencia

Fauntleroy, Gussie. "La Querencia: The Place of Your Heart's Desire."
  New Mexico Magazine, September 1997.

Gruchow, Paul. *The Necessity of Empty Places*. Minneapolis: Milkweed
  Press, 1999.

Muir, John. *My First Summer in the Sierra*. New York: Houghton
  Mifflin, 1911.

O'Connell, Nicholas. "On Sacred Ground." *Sierra*,
  November/December 1998.

Preston, Douglas. *Cities of Gold: A Journey across the American
  Southwest*. Albuquerque: University of New Mexico, 1992.

Turner, Jack. *The Abstract Wild*. Tucson: University of Arizona Press,
  1996.

2. Spirits in the Sandias

Fletcher, Colin. *River: One Man's Journey down the Colorado, Source to
  Sea*. New York: Knopf, 1997.

Roybal, Rebecca. "Urban Camping Exposes Youths to Fun in Safety."
  Albuquerque Journal, 26 October 2001.

Williams, Brooke. *Halflives: Reconciling Work and Wildness*.
  Washington, D.C.: Island Press, 1999.

Turner, Jack. *The Abstract Wild*. Tucson: University of Arizona Press,
  1996.

4. Bandelier National Monument

Bass, Rick. *The Book of Yaak*. Boston: Houghton Mifflin, 1996.

Crawford, Stanley. *A Garlic Testament: Seasons on a Small New Mexico
  Farm*. New York: HarperCollins, 1992.

Elder, John. *Reading the Mountains of Home*. Cambridge, Mass.:
  Harvard University Press, 1998.

Graña, Mari. *Begoso Cabin: A Pecos Country Retreat*. Albuquerque:
  University of New Mexico Press, 1999.

Nealson, Christina. *Living on the Spine: A Woman's Life in the Sangre de
  Cristo Mountains*. Watsonville, Calif.: Papier-Mache Press, 1997.

Thoreau, Henry David. *Walden*. New York: Random House, 1937.

5. Close Encounters of the Furry Kind

Turner, Jack. *Teewinot: A Year in the Teton Range*. New York: St. Martin's Press, 2000.

Williams, Terry Tempest. *Refuge: An Unnatural History of Family and Place*. New York: Vintage Books, 1992.

6. The Magic of the Weminuche

Abbey, Edward. *Desert Solitaire*. New York: Ballantine Books, 1991.

Barcott, Bruce. *The Measure of a Mountain: Beauty and Terror on Mount Rainier*. Seattle: Sasquatch Press, 1997.

Brill, David. *As Far as the Eye Can See: Reflections of an Appalachian Trail Hiker*. Nashville: Rutledge Hill Press, 1990.

Cody, Robin. *Voyage of a Summer Sun: Canoeing the Columbia River*. Seattle: Sasquatch Books, 1995.

Cooper, David J. *Brooks Range Passage*. Seattle: The Mountaineers Books, 1982.

Fletcher, Colin. *The Man Who Walked Through Time*. New York: Vintage Books, 1967.

———. *River: One Man's Journey down the Colorado, Source to Sea*. New York: Knopf, 1997.

———. *The Thousand-Mile Summer*. Berkeley, Calif.: Howell-North Books, 1964.

Gebhardt, Dennis. *A Backpacking Guide to the Weminuche Wilderness in the San Juan Mountains of Colorado*. Durango, Colo.: Basin Reproduction and Printing, 1976.

Peacock, Doug. *Grizzly Years: In Search of the American Wilderness*. New York: Henry Holt, 1990.

Townsend, Chris. *High Summer*. Seattle: Cloudcap Press, 1989.

7. The Gila Wilderness

Jenkins, Mark. "Are We Not Men?" *Outside*, April 2000.

Rawlins, C. L. *Sky's Witness: A Year in the Wind River Range*. New York: Henry Holt, 1993.

8. Technology Just Doesn't Matter

Jardine, Ray. *Beyond Backpacking: Ray Jardine's Guide to Lightweight Hiking: Practical Methods for All Who Love the Out-of-Doors, from Walkers and Backpackers, to Long-distance Hikers*. LaPine, Ore.: AdventureLore Press, 2000.

Sources

————. *The Pacific Crest Trail Hiker's Handbook: Innovative Techniques and Trail Tested Instruction for the Long Distance Hiker.* LaPine, Ore.: AdventureLore Press, 1998.

Steere, Mike. "Wonk on the Wild Side." *Outside*, December 1999.

9. Rambling Along Rainforest Paths

Abbey, Edward. *Down the River.* New York: E. P. Dutton, 1991.

————. *One Life at a Time, Please.* New York: Henry Holt, 1978.

Fromm, Pete. *Indian Creek Chronicles.* New York: Lyons & Burford, 1993.

McPhee, John. *The Control of Nature.* New York: Farrar, Straus & Giroux, 1989.

10. The Red Road

Dillard, Annie. *For the Time Being.* New York: Knopf, 1999.

Preston, Douglas. *Cities of Gold: A Journey across the American Southwest.* Albuquerque: University of New Mexico, 1992.

Stuart, David. *Anasazi America.* Albuquerque: University of New Mexico Press, 2000.

11. Circumambulating the Giant Strawberry

Hanscom, Greg. "Bringing Back the Bosque." *High Country News,* 19 November 2001.

Watts, Alan. *Cloud-Hidden, Whereabouts Unknown; A Mountain Journal.* New York: Vintage Books, 1974.